Breaking the String

A Play

Frank Vickery

A SAMUEL FRENCH ACTING EDITION

SAMUEL FRENCH

FOUNDED 1830

SAMUELFRENCH-LONDON.CO.UK
SAMUELFRENCH.COM

FOR AMATEUR PRODUCTION ENQUIRIES

UNITED KINGDOM AND WORLD EXCLUDING NORTH AMERICA

plays@SamuelFrench-London.co.uk

020 7255 4302/01

Each title is subject to availability from Samuel French,

depending upon country of performance.

BREAKING THE STRING

First produced at the Stephen Joseph Theatre-in-the-Round, Scarborough, on 5th March, 1979, and subsequently at the Edinburgh Fringe Festival, with the following cast of characters:

Iris	Christine Tuckett
Ron	Frank Vickery
Simon	Brian Meadows
Deryn	Lorraine John

Directed by Brian Meadows
Stage managed by Deryn Grigg
Designed by Parc and Dare Theatre Company
Music and lighting by John Nagle

It was seen on 13th August, 1989, at the Duke of York's Theatre, London with the following cast:

Iris	Christine Tuckett
Ron	Frank Vickery
Simon	Brian Meadows
Deryn	Lorraine John

Directed by Brian Meadows
Stage managed by Lisa Dawe
Lighting by Alan "Flash" Lewis

CHARACTERS

Iris
Ron
Simon
Deryn

The action takes place in the living-room of the family's suburban house

SYNOPSIS OF SCENES

ACT I
SCENE 1 4.15 on a Friday afternoon
SCENE 2 1.35 p.m. the following day

ACT II
SCENE 1 An hour or so later
SCENE 2 Later that evening

Other titles by Frank Vickery
published by Samuel French Ltd

After I'm Gone
All's Fair
Family Planning
A Night on the Tiles
A Night Out
One O'Clock from the House

ACT I

SCENE 1

The living-room of the family's suburban house. Friday, 4.15 p.m.

The room is sparsely furnished but of exquisite taste. The furniture consists of a Dralon high-backed armchair DR and to the left of it is the settee leaving a comfortable space between. At the right hand side of the settee is a small table and on it an ashtray. DL is a small half-moon table on which there are a few books and a large photograph of Simon at the age of six or seven. A mirror hangs on the wall just behind and UL is a door which leads to the hall. There is a Georgian bow window at the back which is curtained with net and draped with heavy velvet hangings. There are a pair of twin Wall lights at each side of the window with shades that match the furniture and hangings. R there is a door that leads to the kitchen and DR at the wall is a bureau with a picture, if possible a "Constable", hanging above

When the CURTAIN rises Iris is perched at the window. Ron is sitting in the armchair smoking his pipe and filling in a crossword

Iris (*after some time*) I don't know why he's late.
Ron (*without looking up*) He's not late. He said not to expect him until five.
Iris (*over her shoulder*) At the latest. Five at the latest you said, he said.
Ron (*glancing at his watch*) It's only just quarter-past four.
Iris He's always early. He never hangs about. He knows I like him home early.
Ron I wish you'd come away from that window.
Iris I want to keep an eye out.
Ron You'll have people talking.
Iris Let them talk. I'm not doing anything wrong. It's not against the law for a mother to look out for her son. (*She turns to Ron*) You're sure he said five o'clock, Ron?

Ron doesn't answer

Ronnie, I'm talking to you.

He looks at her

You're sure Simon said five o'clock?
Ron (*vaguely*) I think so, yes.
Iris (*moving towards him*) You think so? You think so? Why didn't you write it down? That's what it's there for, you know, that little note pad.
Ron What little note pad?

Iris The one by the telephone. Honestly, Ron, honestly! Sometimes I could, (*she makes a face*) sometimes. (*She goes back to the window*) I don't know why he rang on a Thursday anyway. Not nine o'clock on a Thursday. He knows I've got WI on a Thursday. (*A slight pause*) What time is it now, Ron?

Ron (*without looking at his watch*) Just gone quarter-past four.

Iris He was home before this the last time. I remember because I went and had my hair done, and I had only got in half an hour before him. It couldn't have been much later than three o'clock.

Ron Perhaps he had things to do. Or maybe he couldn't get the car started.

Iris There shouldn't be anything wrong with that car. He said he'd only just had it serviced in his last letter.

Ron I only said *maybe* he couldn't get it started. Look, why don't you come and sit down?

Iris No, I can't, I can't. I've got to do something.

Ron Well, come and watch the big hand on the clock move to the twelve then.

Iris It's all right for you to joke about it. (*Going to the mirror*) I haven't seen him for three months.

Ron I haven't, either.

Iris But it's different for you, you're not his mother. (*Checking her hair in the mirror*) Three months and only three letters. You'd think he'd write to his mother more often. Or ring; he doesn't go short of money. He could ring anytime.

Ron He did ring.

Iris Yes, on a Thursday when I'm at WI ... Why a Thursday I'll never know. If he'd written and said he was going to ring it would have been something. I would have put it off, I wouldn't have gone. (*A thought strikes her*) Ron, I hope there isn't anything wrong.

Ron tuts and folds up his paper

Ron I think I'll make a cup of tea.

Iris Oh, no, you don't. (*Pointing to the kitchen*) I've laid everything out in there and I'm not having you mess it all up. You'll wait till Simon comes and we'll all have tea together. It's a good thing it's only salad, anything hot and it would have been spoiled.

Ron It wouldn't surprise me if it's spoiled anyway.

Iris Don't be silly! You can't spoil salad.

Ron It can dry up.

Iris Only if it's been out for hours.

Ron You did lay it out at one o'clock.

Iris It's all right, it's all right. I've covered it with foil. I wish you wouldn't interfere, Ron. (*Crossing to him*) You'd soon snap my head off if I started to tell you how to dig your garden, wouldn't you? Wouldn't you?

Ron (*sighing and shaking his head*) I should never have told you last night. Two o'clock this afternoon would have been plenty of time.

Iris (*moving to the settee*) And I'd have been rushing round like a thing possessed.

Ron (*almost to himself*) You're like that anyway.

Iris You'd like that, wouldn't you? You'd like to see me drill myself into the kitchen floor rushing to prepare a meal for him.

Ron Iris, it's our son who's coming to stay, not Prince Philip.

Iris It's all right for you to joke about it, but I like things to be right when my son comes home. God knows he doesn't see his mother that often, and to get things right I need time. And time is not two o'clock in the afternoon, (*trilling the "R"*) Ronald.

There is a pause in which Iris wanders back up to the window. Ron realizes that his pipe has gone out, strikes a match to relight it. After being at the window for some time Iris bursts into excitement

Here he is! Here he is!

Ron almost jumps out of his chair with the shock

Oh, no, it's not, wrong car. I thought sure that was Simon sitting behind that wheel. It was a car just like his.

Ron (*putting his hand on his chest*) I wish you wouldn't do that, Iris.

Iris Do what?

Ron Shout like that. If I'd suffered with a bad heart you'd have lost me then.

Iris I don't know what's the matter with you. There's no excitement left in you at all.

Ron Not in the afternoon. I usually save it for the night, but by then of course, well, never mind.

Iris gives him a piercing look then turns back to the window

Iris (*a slight pause*) He's had a lovely afternoon for the drive down.

Ron Yes. It's thirsty work driving in this weather. Perhaps he's stopped on the way for a drink.

Iris No, not Simon. He knows I'll be waiting, and he doesn't like to keep me. He knows I'll worry. And he wouldn't drink and drive anyway.

Ron I didn't mean that he'd exceed the limit. Just a half or so to quench his thirst.

Iris I've got plenty to drink here, Ron.

Ron Yes, but it's in the fridge, two hundred miles from where he is.

Iris Well, maybe he's brought a few cans with him. He wouldn't have to stop the car then, would he?

Ron (*giving up*) No, all right then, Iris.

Iris (*still looking out of the window*) You switched his electric blanket on, Ron, didn't you?

Ron makes a face. He has forgotten

Ron Yes.

Iris That's all right then because this weather is deceiving. It's hot, but it's too soon after that cold spell we've had. It's quite nippy in the shade.

Ron I wish you'd come away from there.

Iris Oh, shut up! (*She stretches her neck to see more clearly*) I see they've bumped the car next door, then.

Ron Yes. *She* did it going down a one way street.

Iris (*turning towards him*) If that remark was designed to put me off driving, Ron, you've failed.

Ron And if you drive on Monday the way you drove yesterday, you'll fail too.

Iris That's right; that's what I need; plenty of encouragement.

Ron I've said it before, Iris, and I'll say it again. You won't be able to argue with the examiner the way you argue with me.

Iris Well, you know I can't take direction and drive at the same time.

Ron You're going to have to, on Monday.

Iris looks at him in disgust, then looks away

You're not ready for your test yet, Iris. You still get trouble doing an eight-point turn.

Iris takes the small ashtray from the arm of Ron's chair and empties it in a bin on the far left next to the half-moon table

Iris That's right, make fun. You'll laugh on the other side of your face when I come home with a pass certificate. And what are you going on about? I did it in six last time.

Ron The object is three, Iris.

Iris (*putting the ashtray back on the chair*) Well, you always take me to that narrow street. Why can't you take me to Mount View Road? That's much wider.

Ron Because Mount View Road isn't on the test course. Where I take you, is.

Iris moves left and straightens the carpet with the heel of her shoe

Iris Rosemary Miller passed her test first time, and she only had six lessons.

Ron Iris, after six lessons you still wanted to drive with the handbrake on.

Iris (*sitting on the settee*) Well, time will tell, and Monday's not far off.

Ron (*a slight pause*) You may as well sit back and relax. He's not going to get here any sooner.

There is a long pause in which Iris raps her fingers on the arm of the settee

Iris Fancy ringing on a Thursday. He never rings. The only night of the week I go out and what happens? He rings. He rings and you take the message. You take the message and forget to write it down.

Ron I didn't forget.

Iris Well, whatever you did, you didn't write it down. You're sure you've got all the details, Ron? The time?

Ron Five o'clock.

Iris The day?

Ron Friday.

Iris Are you sure it's this Friday?

Ron (*after thinking about it for a moment*) Friday, tomorrow, he said; yes.

Iris If you've got the wrong weekend, Ron, so help me I'll—I'll ... (*She rushes to her feet*) SShhhhh, there's a car.
Ron It's not——
Iris SShhhh ... (*She listens*) No, it's not him.
Ron I knew.
Iris (*sitting back on the settee*) You're sure your watch isn't slow?
Ron It was right by the one o'clock news.

A slight pause

Iris If he'd stopped, you'd think he'd ring and say.
Ron And say, what?
Iris Well that he'd stopped. And that he'd be late or something.
Ron I've told you before, Iris, you fuss too much.
Iris Well I can't help it; I'm a born worrier.
Ron I didn't say *worry*, I said *fuss*. You'd better watch it, I'm telling you. You know Simon doesn't like it.
Iris I know no such thing.
Ron Yes, you do. You embarrass him.
Iris (*sitting bolt upright*) How dare you? How dare you say I embarrass him?
Ron You do.
Iris When? When would I do such a thing?
Ron All the time. You do it all the time. Every time you fuss. He's not your little boy anymore, you know.
Iris Yes, he is.
Ron Iris, he's twenty-three years old.
Iris Well, he's still my boy and always will be.

The telephone rings in the hall

I'll get it.

Iris rushes out to the hall

(*Off*) Hello? ... Oh hello, Freda. ... Yes, listen! Look, I can't stop now, I'm expecting Simon to ring any minute and I want to keep the line open. ... Yes, all right dear. First thing on Monday after my test. ... Yes I will. 'Bye, then.

Iris comes back into the room

That was Freda ringing for a chat. I told her to ring on Monday. (*She sits back on the settee*) Time's getting on, Ron.
Ron Why don't you read something?
Iris Oh no, I couldn't. I couldn't concentrate.

Not able to settle on the settee, Iris wanders up to the window. Satisfied that Simon is nowhere in sight she wanders down to Ron and peers over his shoulder at his crossword. Ron becomes aware of her presence, looks up slightly and turns his newspaper away from her. Sighing heavily she returns to sit on the settee

Ron (*thinking aloud*) Six letters and seven letters. (*He reads out the clue*) Will grow in your garden; spot.
Iris (*remembering something*) Pickle cabbage.
Ron What?
Iris Pickle cabbage. I've forgotten to get pickle cabbage and you know how much Simon enjoys it.
Ron (*looking at his paper*) I think you're right.
Iris What do you mean you think I'm right? Of course I'm right.
Ron No, no, it fits.
Iris What does?
Ron Six letters and seven. Will grow in your garden, spot. It's pickle cabbage. Spot-pickle, will grow in your garden—cabbage. It's pickle cabbage.

Ron shakes his head and smiles to himself as Iris looks at him aghast

Iris (*with almost a faint touch of concern in her voice*) I think you're doing too many of them crosswords, Ron.

A car horn is heard outside. Iris rushes to the window

It's him. It's Simon, he's here. I said he'd be here before five, didn't I? (*Calling*) Simon! (*She waves to him almost unable to control her excitement. Suddenly she stops. She looks quickly over her shoulder at Ron and then back out of the window. There is something wrong. She is obviously distraught. She comes down to the settee*)

Ron senses something and looks at her

Ron What's the matter?
Iris Nothing.
Ron Is there something wrong?
Iris No, nothing.
Ron Why did you——?
Iris (*sharply*) I said there's nothing.

Two car doors are heard slamming and a few seconds later the doorbell chimes. Ron, who is looking at his newspaper, looks up

Ron Aren't you going to answer it?
Iris No, you.
Ron I thought you'd want to ...
Iris Well, you thought wrong, didn't you?

The doorbell chimes again, longer this time

Answer it, Ron, before he runs the batteries down.

Ron gets up and goes to the hall

Ron (*off*) Hello, son. Hello.
Simon (*off*) Hello, Dad.
Ron (*off*) Don't stand at the door. Come in. Come on, come in.

Meanwhile, Iris has taken Ron's newspaper and sits far left on the settee

Simon hesitantly enters the room. He comes C

Simon Hello, Mum.

Iris looks up from the newspaper and forces a smile

Iris Simon. (*She returns to her reading*)

Simon looks to the hall door and motions for someone to come in

A few seconds later Deryn enters, followed by Ron

Simon Mum, I'd like you to meet Deryn.
Iris (*without looking up from the newspaper*) You've lost weight.
Simon No, I haven't.
Iris Yes, you have. You've lost weight. (*She looks at him*) I thought you
might have rung. You might have rung and said something.
Simon Deryn, this is my mum.
Deryn Hello.

Iris returns to her paper

Simon And my dad.

Deryn smiles sweetly

Ron Hello, love. Well, don't let's stand. Come on! Let's sit down.

*Simon seats Deryn in the armchair and Ron motions to Simon to sit next to his
mother on the settee. Ron stands next to Deryn. There is a pause*

Deryn I hope I haven't left the suitcases in anyone's way.
Iris (*to Simon*) Suitcases?
Deryn (*looking quickly at Simon then at Iris*) I've left them in the hall.
Simon Deryn's staying, Mum.
Iris Is she?
Simon You don't mind?

*Iris gives Simon a piercing look before going back to her paper. Ron tries to
cover the embarrassment*

Ron I'll take them upstairs then.

Ron goes

Deryn (*to Iris*) If it's not convenient . . .?
Iris (*to Simon*) You could have rung and said, Simon. At least you could
have rung and said.
Simon I wanted to surprise you.
Deryn I said it wouldn't be convenient. (*To Simon*) Didn't I?
Simon (*to Deryn*) It's all right. (*To Iris*) Isn't it?
Iris I haven't got the spare room ready.
Simon Oh, I see. Well OK then. (*He gets up*)
Iris Where are you going?
Simon If there's no room for Deryn then there's no room for me either.

Iris Now, I never said there wasn't room. I only said it wasn't ready.
Simon With you, Mum, that means the same thing.
Iris Go and tell your father to put an electric blanket in the spare room; go
on.

Simon smiles at her then at Deryn, then leaves the room

*Deryn looks around the room while Iris stares at her. Eventually their eyes
meet*

You haven't known him long, then?
Deryn Oh, we've known each other about a year, but it wasn't until a few
months ago that we ...
Iris What?
Deryn Well, started to see more of each other.
Iris It surprises me how he's got time to see you at all. He led me to believe
that his fourth year was pretty strenuous.
Deryn Oh it is, but all work and no play ...

Iris stands and goes to the mirror

Iris I suppose you want to be a doctor, too?
Deryn Me? (*She laughs*) God, no!
Iris (*patting her hair*) So you're not at the same college then?
Deryn No.
Iris So where did you meet?
Deryn In a laundrette.
Iris (*disgusted*) You work in a laundrette?
Deryn (*laughing*) No, of course not.
Iris (*almost afraid to ask*) What is it exactly you do?
Deryn I'm an artist. I draw and paint and sculpt things.
Iris What things?
Deryn People mostly.
Iris Thank God for that! I thought for a moment that you were one of those
modern art creatures who paints all those odd shapes and colours and
then calls them beautiful.
Deryn No, I'm pretty conventional I'm afraid. I did an abstract once, when
I was in my first year. But it wasn't my idea of beauty.
Iris I suppose that's what drew you to Simon.
Deryn I beg your pardon?
Iris Well, if you like drawing people and him being so, well, it embarrasses
me to say it. I shouldn't. I should be proud and I am. I mean, he can't help
being so handsome, can he? There I've said it.
Deryn (*slightly embarrassed*) Yes, he is rather nice, isn't he?
Iris (*taking Simon's photograph from the table*) Of course, his father was.
I'm not ashamed to say it but he does take after his father. (*Sitting on the
settee*) The times, you'd never believe the times people would come up to
me when he was a baby and say how pretty he was. Too pretty for a boy
they'd say. And of course he hasn't changed. He's still the same as he was.
Except that he's lost weight, but a week home, a week home with his

mother's cooking and he'll be as right as rain. (*Handing Deryn the photograph*) There you are, that's little Simon.

Deryn Only he's not so little now, is he?

Iris Still as pretty though.

Deryn (*looking at the photograph*) I think handsome is the word.

Iris It means the same thing.

Deryn But it doesn't, it——

Iris (*snapping*) Pardon, dear?

Deryn (*after a slight pause*) Pretty is usually associated with the female sex.

Iris (*taken aback*) You may as well know it now, dear——

Deryn My name is Deryn.

Iris Well you may as well know it now, I don't allow talk like that in this house.

Deryn Talk like what?

Iris Like you said. That word

Deryn (*after thinking for a moment*) Sex?

Iris (*firmly*) I said I don't allow it.

Deryn God, you're not real!

Iris How dare you! How dare you call me that!

Deryn (*hastily apologetic*) All right, I'm sorry.

Iris (*walking towards the window*) I should think you are. Honestly! The youngsters these days.

Deryn Please! Don't let's row.

Iris I'm old enough to be your mother.

Deryn I've said I'm sorry.

Iris (*turning towards her*) I should think you are. I should think you are sorry.

Deryn It's just that you keep referring to him——

Iris Why shouldn't I refer to him?

Deryn (*standing*) Please, let me finish. You keep referring to him with all the wrong words. He's not little anymore, and he's certainly not pretty.

Iris is about to speak but Deryn carries on

Handsome, yes, but not pretty. He's not as you see him at all.

Iris Who do you think you are? What do you think gives you the right to tell me how to see my own son?

Deryn almost tells her, but doesn't

Deryn Please, don't let's go on. I'm sure Simon wouldn't like it.

Iris (*taking the photograph from her*) Finished with that have you? (*She puts it back on the table*)

Deryn Look, I didn't want to come this weekend.

Iris Why did you then?

Deryn Because Simon asked me.

Iris Is it so difficult to say "no" to him?

Deryn As a matter of fact, it is. I don't think I could ever say "no" to him. No matter what he asked.

Iris I see. So it's like that, is it?

Deryn I'm sure you know what it feels like.

Iris looks at her

What I mean is, (*taking two small steps towards her*) I don't think you can say "no" to him either. Not easily anyway.

Iris You don't know what I think. I'm his mother and that's something you'll never be.

Deryn (*turning away slightly*) And something I'll never want to be.

Iris Don't be so condescending.

Deryn (*biting her tongue*) I'm sorry, I didn't mean to be.

Iris You're so condescending.

Deryn Look, I'm trying for Simon's sake. Why can't you?

Iris (*crossing behind the settee and standing to the side of the armchair*) You'll be a mother yourself one day. God forbid! Then you'll know what it's all about. People, young people have no conception of what it's like to be a mother these days. Not a good mother, any way.

Deryn True, perhaps. So the only thing young people can do, is learn from older people's mistakes.

Iris You think you're very clever, don't you?

Deryn All I want is to——

Iris I've met your type before. An answer for everything, I know. Think you know it all, don't you?

Deryn If you want me to leave, I will.

Iris You'd like that, wouldn't you? You'd like to leave knowing that Simon wants you to stay. Then you can blame it on me. Tell him I didn't make you welcome.

Deryn I won't have to tell him that.

Iris looks at her

He's not blind. He could see as well as we all could, that you weren't in love with the idea of me staying.

Iris Well you won't leave. I'm not having Simon think it's me. (*Sitting in the armchair*) You'll stay, and you'll stay just as long as Simon wants you to.

Deryn Oh no, you've got it all wrong. I'll stay until I'm ready to leave.

Iris I thought you said you couldn't say "no" to him? I thought you didn't mean it. It didn't ring true somehow when you said it.

Deryn When I said it, I didn't reckon on *you*. I'm not going to fight you. I won't let myself.

Iris Why?

Deryn Because there's nothing to fight for.

Iris Rubbish. You're afraid you'll lose.

Deryn No I'm not. (*Meaningfully*) I've already won.

Iris What do you mean? What do you mean you've already won?

Simon comes into the room followed by Ron

Simon Right, let's have tea, I'm starved. I've put your suitcase in your bedroom, Der, OK?

Deryn I'll go and unpack then.

Simon It's all right, leave it till later.

Deryn No. (*Glancing slightly towards Iris*) I'd rather do it now. Which room am I in?

Simon It's the front one. Come on, I'll show you.

They are about to leave the room

Iris Don't be long.

Simon I'm only going to show Deryn her room.

Iris raises one eyebrow. They start to leave but again Iris stops them

Iris Aren't you forgetting something?

Simon looks at her, then at Deryn. Iris puts her cheek out towards him

Something you should have done when you came in.

Simon looks embarrassed

Come on, Simon, welcome me like you used to. It's terrible I should have to remind you. Only one mother you'll have, you know. Come on.

Simon reluctantly crosses and kisses her

Huh, I don't know why you bothered. A fine greeting after not seeing me for three months.

Simon Look, I——

Iris Go on. Show her the room, go on.

Simon looks at Ron. Ron nods for him to show Deryn her room

Simon and Deryn leave

Ron comes to sit on the settee and picks up the newspaper

Ron If you're not careful, Iris, you'll blow it once and for all.

Iris Don't you start! It's hard enough having to cope with this lot without having you start.

Ron Having to cope with what?

Iris Don't play the innocent with me. You knew all this was coming, didn't you?

Ron I don't know what you're talking about.

Iris I suppose he told you yesterday.

Ron Told me what?

Iris You're not going to try and tell me that he never mentioned this little lot when he rang yesterday?

Ron I can't make you believe me.

Iris He must have mentioned it; he must have. (*She waits for some sort of statement from Ron, but nothing is forthcoming*) Ron, I said he must have.

Ron Well he didn't.

Iris You wouldn't give him away, anyway, if he did. You're as deep as he is. Always have been and always will be. You're like the Pacific—the pair of you.

Ron Look, if I were you I'd start being nice. I know it's going to be difficult for you——

Iris I'd clarify that last remark if I were you. Just because I haven't taken to her——

Ron Haven't taken to her? The hair on the back of your neck stood on end the minute you saw her step out of the car. I'm warning you, Iris, you've never been one who's able to hide your feelings. Simon can see how you are, and I'm sure Deryn can, too.

Iris I'm only looking after his interests.

Ron looks at her

I wanted him to qualify before he started getting friendly with girls. There's plenty of time for that sort of thing later.

Ron Well, you can make up your mind. Here you are talking about looking after his interests, wanting him to qualify. I almost had to break every bone in your body to get you to agree to let him go to medical school.

Iris Yes, but that was a long time ago. It wasn't easy for me to let him go I'll admit, but I did, and I'm not having a young slip of a girl ruin it all.

Ron You're jumping the gun a bit, aren't you?

Iris I'm a woman, Ron. I can tell. She's got designs on him in no uncertain terms.

Ron What if she has? There's no harm in it. Iris—he's twenty-three, over and above the age of consent. He and Deryn can do whatever they like and there isn't anything that you or I or anybody can do about it.

Iris I might have known you'd take his part. You see everything his way.

Ron He's not stupid, Iris. He never has been. Give him credit for that. Trust him.

Iris Trust? Huh, trust went out of the window the day they invented the pill. (*Coming to sit next to Ron on the settee*) Do you know where he met her? In a laundrette. A laundrette! I ask you.

Ron I met you in an air raid shelter.

Iris I always said he should have sent his washing home.

Ron She seems a nice girl.

Iris She's an artist, she told me. She draws and paints things.

Ron And if you're not nice to her she'll leave.

Iris I'm sure I won't waste any tears.

Ron And if she does, Simon will leave with her.

Iris No he won't.

Ron Yes, he will.

Iris No, he won't.

Ron Yes, he will.

Iris How do you know, has he told you?

Ron No.

Iris Well, there you are then.

Ron (*after a slight pause*) Be nice to her, Iris. For Simon's sake.

Iris Listen to you and everyone would think I've been a right dragon. Just because I didn't fall over backwards . . .

Ron No-one's asking you to do that. (*A slight pause*) I think you'd better be nice to her, Iris.

Iris Why? Do you know something I don't?

Ron I doubt it.

Iris I get the feeling that ... well ... that there's something going on. And I'm the only one not part of it.

Ron You're paranoid.

Iris No, Ron, I'm right. I've had a distinct urge.

Ron I know the feeling. Take a tip and suppress it.

Iris I don't think I like it.

Ron That's what you always say.

Iris (*looking at him*) Pardon?

Ron Nothing.

A slight pause

Iris You're quite sure he never mentioned her on the telephone?

Ron Her name is Deryn.

Iris Yes, all right. You're sure he didn't mention her yesterday?

Ron Positive.

Iris (*walking past the armchair far right*) He's brought her home for a reason. There's a reason for it, I'm sure.

Ron Perhaps it's because he wants to show her off.

Iris Why on earth would he want to do that?

Ron She's very pretty. He's feeling proud. I think he wants us to be, too.

Iris Proud of what?

Ron His choice.

Iris She's an artist.

Ron It doesn't matter what she is, she's Simon's choice, and he wants our approval, I think.

Iris You don't think, Ron, you know. He's told you, hasn't he?

Ron No.

Iris You ought to be struck dead. He's told you, he must have.

Ron The boy hasn't been home twenty minutes, what's the matter with you?

Iris I'm not talking about now. I'm talking about last night on the telephone.

Ron Look, I've already told you. You've made me repeat it four times. All he said was that he was coming home today and not to expect him till five.

Iris At the latest. Five at the latest.

Ron Well, there you are then. That's it, word for word.

Iris (*advancing towards Ron but coming to stand behind the settee*) I'll find out. I'll find out what's going on. Sooner or later I'll find out.

Ron Well perhaps in the meantime we can have some tea?

Iris Trust you to think about your stomach at a time like this.

Ron I'm not thinking about my stomach. It's Simon who said he was starved.

Iris Yes, and I'm sorry it's salad now. From what I can see of him he could do with a few cooked dinners inside him.

Ron Now don't start fussing.

Iris Fussing? Fussing? I'm telling you, Ron, when Simon walked in here my heart turned over in my chest. The weight that boy's lost.

Ron Don't be ridiculous.

Iris Ridiculous am I? I'm telling you, I've seen more weight on my kitchen scales.

Ron Leave the boy alone.

Iris He can't carry on like that. There'll be nothing left of him.

Ron He looks the same to me as he did when he came home for Christmas.

Iris (*going back to sit in the armchair*) You can say what you like, Ron, that boy hasn't been eating. And he's burning the candle at both ends, too, I expect.

Ron Well you're only young once.

Iris That's always your answer for everything where Simon is concerned, isn't it?

Ron I'm not going to argue with you, Iris.

Iris No, I know. Sometimes, Ron, honestly, sometimes I think an argument would do you good.

Ron No it wouldn't. I don't like arguments.

Iris (*shouting*) Well it would do me good then.

A slight pause

Ron (*sitting forward on the settee*) All I'm saying is that Simon has come home for a holiday. He's brought a girl with him. I think we should make her feel welcome. Iris? Please?

Iris (*turning towards him*) I think you'd better go and put the kettle on.

Ron sighs and goes out to the kitchen as Simon enters

Simon sees Iris sitting in the chair. He turns and looks at his reflection in the mirror

Simon I've changed rooms with Deryn, Mum.

Iris sits up

She can't sleep with the street lights on.

Iris How do you know?

Simon She told me. (*He sits on the settee. There is a pause*) I didn't tell you about Deryn because——

Iris How are you then?

Simon I'm all right.

Iris Just all right?

Simon No I'm fine. I'm great.

There is a pause

Iris I'm very well, thank you very much.

Simon About Deryn——

Iris Where is she anyway?

Simon She's upstairs, freshening up. I wanted her to be a surprise.

Iris Well, she was certainly that.

Simon Are you still annoyed?

Iris (*melting a little*) I dare say I'll come round.

Simon (*smiling*) I hoped you would.

They look at each other

I didn't tell you about Deryn because I knew you'd fuss. Lay everything on. Best telephone voice and all that.

Iris So that's what you think of me?

Simon But you would have though, wouldn't you?

Iris I dare say I would have gone to a little more trouble I expect. That spare room would have been re-decorated for a start.

Simon And that's what I don't want. I don't want you to fuss. (*After a short pause*) You're looking well, Mum.

Iris Well I don't feel it. I'm a bag of nerves. (*She pauses*) How's everything at school?

Simon OK. It's uphill all the way.

Iris Success always is.

Simon I feel like throwing it all in sometimes.

Iris You can't do that. Not with only two years to go.

Simon After this year.

Iris You can't give it up, Simon, you can't.

Simon I only said I felt like it sometimes.

Iris I've told everybody you're going to be a doctor. I'll never be able to show my face in the surgery again. I hope she hasn't got anything to do with all this?

Simon Her name is Deryn.

Iris Has she?

Simon (*after a slight pause, standing*) Where's tea? I'm starved.

Iris I expect you are. (*Also standing*) I bet you're glad to come home for a decent meal.

Simon The food's all right where I am.

Iris (*pinching his tummy*) Well, why don't you eat it then?

Simon I do. I eat well.

Iris Looking the way you do? You've lost at least half a stone since Christmas.

Simon I'm the same weight now as I've always been.

Iris When did you weigh last, then? Come on, tell me. When did you weigh last?

Simon Five minutes ago in the bathroom. And I'm exactly the same weight as I was yesterday.

Iris Yes, well, those scales are at least six pounds out.

Simon (*taking Iris by both hands*) Look, Mother——

Deryn comes into the room

I'm ten stone four. I'm in perfect health, and I'm hungry.

Deryn (*coming down to the left of Simon*) Snap, I'm not ten stone four but I am starved.

Iris (*to Simon*) Your father has put the kettle on.

Ron comes in from the kitchen

Ron Come on, then, it's all ready for you.
Simon Good.
Iris I think you'd better make up some mash potato, Ron.
Ron Yes, I already have.

Iris makes a face because Ron has already thought of it

Simon Deryn?

Simon offers Deryn his arm. She takes it and they both walk with exaggerated grandeur between Iris and Ron and go out to the kitchen

When Simon and Deryn have gone, Ron offers the same to Iris

Ron (*offering his arm*) Iris?
Iris Honestly, Ron, (*walking past him*), honestly, sometimes I think you're as dull as he is.

She goes out to the kitchen leaving Ron to follow sheepishly behind

Black-out

SCENE 2

The same. The next day, 1.35 p.m.

When the Lights come up, Iris is perched again the Georgian bow. She is hugging a cup of tea

Iris I don't know; I seem to spend half my life waiting for that boy. He said he'd be back by one and look at the time. (*She looks at her watch*) Twenty to two.
Ron (*off, from the kitchen*) You're five minutes fast.
Iris (*moving to the armchair*) All right, twenty-five to then, he's still late. (*Standing between the armchair and bureau*) For two pins I'd turn that coc-au-vin off.

Ron comes in from the kitchen wearing a plastic apron. He is drying two or three tea plates with a tea towel

Ron I already have.
Iris What did you do that for?
Ron They can always re-heat it, later, if they fancy it.
Iris You could have given it until two o'clock. I was going to wait until two o'clock and then I was going to turn it off.
Ron Well it's done now and that's that. Can I have that cup?
Iris No.
Ron I'm waiting to finish the dishes.
Iris I'll wash it later.

Ron goes back into the kitchen

Iris sips her tea and goes back to the window. After she is satisfied that Simon is nowhere in sight she wanders aimlessly around the room. Eventually she comes to sit on the settee

She doesn't like me, you know *(She raises her voice a little)* I said that girl, that Keryn or Feryn or whatever her name is. I said she doesn't like me. I knew straight away as soon as she walked through that door last night, I knew. I'm very quick like that. *(She sips her tea)* I don't know what I've done to her, I'm sure. You know what she told me? She said I refer to Simon with all the wrong words. With all the wrong *words*. Made me feel as if I had a small vocabulary. With all the wrong words, that's what she said. Honestly, the cheek of it. I know what she's up to though. I told her last night when you and Simon were upstairs. "I know what your game is," I said. She threatened to leave, you see. After she told me that Simon would be offended if she went of course. But she wasn't going to put the blame on me. I wasn't going to have Simon blame me if she went.

The doorbell chimes

I'll get it.

Iris goes out to the hall as Ron comes in from the kitchen

Ron sits in the armchair DR, *takes out his pipe and smokes it*

Deryn enters a few seconds later, followed sheepishly by Iris

Simon's not with you then?
Deryn No, he's still down at Roger's. He shouldn't be too long, though.
Iris Roger's?
Deryn Yes, Roger Slate——
Iris I know who he is, thank you very much.
Deryn *(sitting on the settee)* We met him and his wife down at the *Swan*. They made ever such a fuss. Simon and I didn't really want to go back to their place but they insisted. She's a fabulous cook you know, his wife. We said we had to be back by one but they practically forced us to stay for lunch.
Iris Oh, so you've already eaten then?
Deryn Mmmmm. It was delicious too. She said it was something that she quickly threw together. Threw together! It must have taken all of an hour and a half. Still it was worth it though. You know I think it was the best coq-au-vin I've ever tasted.

Ron almost chokes on his pipe. Deryn sees Iris's reaction

We didn't put you out or anything, did we? I mean nothing spoiled or anything?

Iris doesn't answer

You didn't wait before having yours, did you?
Iris *(with false charm, almost sarcastic)* No, no, of course not. When it came to quarter past one we could see that you weren't coming so we went ahead and had ours.

Ron looks at her amazed at the bare faced lie. Iris fixes him with a glare

Deryn Oh, that's all right then. Excuse me, won't you, I'm just going up to my room.

Deryn goes

Iris (*advancing towards Ron*) If you let on to her or Simon that we had coq-au-vin for lunch, your life won't be worth living. (*Sitting on settee*) Two hours you slaved in that kitchen and for what? To be told that they've eaten out, and if that wasn't good enough, she had to top it by telling me they had coq-au-vin.
Ron It wasn't Deryn's fault they had coq-au-vin.
Iris Oh, shut up.
Ron I told you to make something different.
Iris Coq-au-vin is different.
Ron Like fricassee or something.
Iris And he likes chicken. Simon likes chicken.
Ron That's easier to re-heat.
Iris There are fifty-two chicken dishes in that cookbook I bought you, Ron. Fifty-two. I choose one of them and what happens? The whole town decides to cook coq-au-vin.
Ron It was only Roger's wife.
Iris Shut up, I said. If I didn't know better I'd say she did it on purpose.
Ron I've said it before, Iris, and I'll say it again, you're paranoid.
Iris (*hurt*) How dare you!
Ron You are; you're paranoid. Obsessed by the girl.
Iris I'm no such thing.
Ron They decided to eat out, for goodness sake. There's nothing wrong in that. You heard her say yourself that Roger and his wife were forceful. Even that's understandable; they haven't seen Simon for months.
Iris That makes three of us.
Ron And it's the first time for them to meet Deryn. They probably had a lot to talk about.
Iris (*meaningfully*) I bet they did.
Ron And what do you mean by that?
Iris Nothing.
Ron Iris, you've never said anything that didn't mean anything.
Iris I don't know what you're talking about.
Ron Then explain what you meant.
Iris About what?
Ron Not what; who.
Iris Who, then?
Ron Simon and Deryn.
Iris Now who's obsessed by her?
Ron (*giving up*) All right, Iris, forget it. But let's do just that and not mention it again.

Iris Well, don't you mention the coq-au-vin, then. If they find out, Ron, I'll
know who's told them.

Ron Of course you'll know who's told them since I'm the only other person
living here.

Iris Well, just remember what I said. There are some people, and I'm not
going to mention any names, but there are some people who would in all
probability see a funny side to all this if she was told, and believe me that
will be the last straw as far as I'm concerned. I'd never have any looks on
her if she turned around after all this and laughed at my cold coq-au-vin.

Ron I thought we weren't going to talk about it anymore.

Iris I'm not. (*A pause*) I was just explaining that's all that——

Ron Iris?

She stops and looks at him

Shut up!

*She stares at him with her bottom lip quivering. Ron sees that she is about to
cry*

You're not going to get upset are you?

Iris (*almost crying*) No.

Ron I couldn't stand it, if you got upset.

Iris (*wiping the corner of her eyes*) I'm not, I'm not, I'm not going to get
upset. I wouldn't let you upset me anyway.

Ron I've said it now.

Iris Thirty-two years I've been married to you. Thirty-two years and you've
never spoken to me like that before.

Ron Well, Iris, after thirty-two years it's about time I did.

Iris That's her though, isn't it?

Ron Who?

Iris Her upstairs.

Ron Now, you know what we've said.

Iris Well, she must have got something to do with it, because you've never
spoken to me like that before, and she's not in the house twenty-four
hours when you're raising your voice at me.

Ron I raised my voice at you because you were going on and on about this
coq-au-vin thing.

The doorbell chimes

Iris (*going to the mirror and drying her eyes*) That's probably Simon. Go and
answer the door, Ron.

*Ron goes out and eventually Simon comes into the room followed by Ron.
Simon spreads himself on the settee. Ron sits in his usual chair*

Simon Sorry I'm late, Mum—only we bumped into Roger and——

Iris Yes, I've heard all about it.

Simon Where's Deryn?

No-one answers at first. Then Iris speaks

Iris She's upstairs.

Simon We had a smashing lunch.

Iris So I'm told. Coq-au-vin, wasn't it?

Simon Yes, that's right.

Iris It's a good thing you stayed then. Your father and I only had something quick.

Simon Oh, good. I'm glad you didn't go to the trouble of making anything special. What did you have?

Iris (*a little lost for words*) Oh it was only, er, something I quickly threw together. Fricassee.

Simon Fricassee? Any left?

Iris Er ...

Simon We'll re-heat it and have it for supper if that's all right?

Iris (*unsure*) Yes.

Simon Deryn raved over Jill's coq-au-vin, and it really was delicious, but I told her she hasn't tasted yours yet.

Iris beams

That's really something special.

Iris Would you like me to make some?

Simon Pardon?

Iris Coq-au-vin. Would you like me to make some?

Simon Well, yes.

Iris (*crossing behind the settee*) I've got plenty of chicken portions in the freezer.

Simon Perhaps we could have it before——

Iris If I go and prepare it now we can have it for tea.

Ron I doubt if they'll want it for tea, Iris, not having just had it for lunch.

Iris Shut up, Ron. The boy has asked for coq-au-vin and coq-au-vin he shall have.

Simon I was going to suggest it for Monday. Before we leave.

Iris You're leaving on Monday?

Simon nods

But you always stay home for a few weeks.

Simon I can't this time. I've got things to catch up on.

Iris You're not behind with your studying, are you?

Simon Well I need to——

Iris Didn't I say it? Didn't I say he'd never be able to keep up his studying and go out with girls?

Simon I want to decorate——

Iris It all comes back to her, doesn't it? Everything comes back to her all the time.

Simon No—I want to——

Iris (*to Simon*) I told you yesterday. Didn't I tell you?

Simon (*raising his voice*) I want to decorate my room.

Iris (*after a slight pause*) Pardon?

Simon I do have some studying to do but I'm not behind. (*To Ron*) I'm not behind, Dad.

There is a pause

Iris What time will you be leaving on Monday?

Simon Not early.

Iris I've got my driving test on Monday. It would be nice if you're here when I get back.

Simon Probably after lunch. Yes, we'll leave after lunch.

Iris Let me see now, then. My test is at eleven; it is at eleven, isn't it, Ron?

Ron nods

Yes I thought it was. I've got an hour's lesson before, plus the drive to the centre. If I prepare it all before breakfast it should be ready for one.

Ron So it's coq-au-vin for four at one o'clock on Monday then?

Iris Yes.

Ron Just as long as we know.

Simon And if you pass, Mum, we'll get a bottle of wine to celebrate.

Iris There's no "if" about it, Simon. I'm going there on Monday to come back with a pass certificate.

Simon What do you reckon her chances are, Dad?

Iris looks at Ron

Ron Oh, so-so.

She smiles at Simon. Immediately Ron shakes his head and Iris catches a glimpse of this

Iris And when I've passed, Simon, we'll be able to come up some weekends and see you. You'd like that, wouldn't you?

Simon (*not at all convinced*) Yes. (*He looks at Ron for some sort of help*)

Iris I thought you would.

Ron It's a long way, you know.

Iris It's only four hours' driving.

Ron For me, yes, but for you it means staying overnight.

Iris Well, we can do that too. I'm sure there are some lovely bed and breakfast places up there, aren't there, Simon?

Simon tries to smile in agreement

It would be a nice break for me to have a weekend away. I've got a better idea. (*She joins Simon on the settee*) Why don't you leave decorating your room? That way you can stay here longer, and your father and I will come up in a couple of weeks, and do it for you.

Simon That's very kind of you, Mum, but——

Ron (*to Iris*) You've never decorated a room in your life.

Iris I've helped, though.

Ron Only last month I finished decorating this house from top to bottom except——

Iris Except the spare room.

Ron I was just about to say except the spare room. Frankly I've had enough of decorating for a while.

Simon (*to Iris*) Look, I'm very grateful but I want to do it myself. The others have to do it so why not me?

Iris If I'd known you were that keen on painting and decorating I would never have sent you to medical school.

Simon in a rage of frustration gets up and goes to the window

Well what have I said now?

Ron As usual, Iris, too much.

Iris (*standing*) Well, it comes to something if I can't speak my own mind in my own house.

She goes upstairs, slamming the living-room door behind her

Simon I think she's upset.

Ron No, she does that for effect.

Simon I've only been home a day and already I can't wait to leave.

A slight pause

Ron Cup of something?

Simon No thanks, Dad. (*Moving slightly towards Ron*) You won't let her come up and see us, will you?

Ron Not if I can stop her.

Simon It's not that I don't want to see her. It's just that if she did, she'd take over.

Ron I know.

Simon My life wouldn't be my own again.

Ron I know, I know.

Simon I'd like to see you, of course.

Ron Never mind, you can ring me.

Simon (*laughing*) Yes, on a Thursday.

Ron (*laughing*) Yes, she still hasn't got over that, you know.

Simon (*moving* DL *in front of the settee*) Me ringing?

Ron She made me repeat everything at least four times.

Simon You didn't tell her anything, did you?

Ron What do you think? She wouldn't be anything like she is now if she had any kind of an idea.

Simon True. God, I'm glad I've got you on my side.

Ron That's what fathers are for.

Simon I hope I'll make half the father you are.

Ron smiles

Ron When do you intend telling her?

Simon I don't know. Some time tonight.

Ron Well, I suggest about the ten o'clock mark.

Simon Why's that?

Ron She takes two Librium at nine.

Simon (*laughing*) Can't you slip her a double dose?

Ron (*laughing*) No such luck.

Simon It's going to be awful for you afterwards, isn't it?

Ron shrugs his shoulders

I mean, it'll be OK for us, we'll be hundreds of miles away.

Ron It's nothing I haven't gone through before. I'm used to it now. We probably won't sleep for three or four weeks but she'll get over it. It'll ruin her driving test, of course, but she was going to fail that anyway.

Simon I suppose I could leave it and say nothing.

Ron You may as well tell her now and get it over with. She's bound to find out eventually.

Simon Yes, you're right. I just thought, maybe, if I postpone it . . .

Ron "Hell" it's going to be whether she's told now or next year.

Simon It may as well be tonight, then.

Ron At sometime after nine.

There is a pause in which Simon looks at his father

Simon I suppose you think I've made a mess of things?

Ron Not really. You're not coming out of college, are you?

Simon (*sitting on left of settee*) No. It's important for us that I qualify and get my degree.

Ron It's not going to be easy, financially.

Simon No, I know. I've already found someone who will buy the car. (*A thought strikes him*) You don't mind me selling it, do you?

Ron (*shaking his head*) Don't be silly.

Simon Only you bought it for me and——

Ron It's all right.

Simon looks at Ron and Ron winks at him. Simon smiles

There's no need for you to worry about money. I'll send you something once a month or so.

Simon We should be able to manage all right. Deryn's quite a good artist. Well, she's more of an impressionist really. She sells quite a bit.

Ron What's this flat that you've got like then?

Simon Oh, it's not much, but when it's decorated . . .

Ron Is there hot water?

Simon A geyser.

Ron nods. There is a slight pause

Ron Will you let me send the rent to you?

Simon We should be able to manage that. It's not that much anyway. I'd rather you send something when we need you to. I won't be afraid to ask you to help me, I mean *us*, when we need it.

Ron So you're all fixed up, then? Nothing you need?

Simon I don't think so.

Ron Right. (*He stands*) Shall we go to the nursery, then?

Simon Nursery?

Ron The garden nursery. I want to get a couple of conifers for the front lawn.

Simon Oh, yes, of course, I forgot. We're going there this afternoon, aren't we?

Ron There are one or two other shrubs I want to get while we're there, as well.

Simon Dad? You haven't told me what you think of Deryn.

Ron Is that a question?

Simon Yes.

Ron Well, it's not a fair one.

Simon In what way?

Ron Well, I mean, she's yours, isn't she? If you'd walked in here with a gorgon I'd have thought she was lovely.

They both laugh

No, seriously, she's very nice.

Simon I knew you'd like her.

Ron You'll have to give your mother time.

Simon How long do you reckon?

Ron Difficult to say. Could be months, could be years.

Simon Do you think she'll ever forgive me for growing up?

Ron I doubt it.

Simon Then I doubt if she'll ever forgive Deryn for taking me away from her.

Ron But she didn't, did she? You were taken, or rather, sent, a long time before Deryn came along.

Simon I know that and you know it, but no way under the sun is "Mater" going to accept it.

Ron She's going to have to. What's done is done. All that's left to do now is make the best——

Simon Of a bad job?

Ron Is that how you feel about it?

Simon No. I didn't want it to happen this way. I didn't plan it, it just did. But I don't regret it. Deryn is everything to me as far as I'm concerned. I love her, Dad. She's right for me.

Ron Then you've got nothing in the world to worry about.

Deryn comes into the room

Deryn (*to Simon*) Oh you're back, then?

Simon Yes, I left just after you did.

Deryn I've just had a lovely shower.

Simon I'll have mine when I get back.

Deryn Where are you off to?

Simon To the garden nursery. Want to come?

Deryn No, thanks. I want to do a few sketches of the house.

Ron (*standing*) This house?

Deryn (*nodding*) And the garden. I want to do some of the garden too.

Simon And she does portraits.

Deryn (*to Ron*) I'll do yours, if you like.

Ron Yes, I'd like that. I've never had anything like that done before.

Deryn I hope you won't be too disappointed. I'm not that good.

Simon Don't listen to her. She's superb.

Ron I'm sure it'll be excellent.

Deryn When you get back from the nursery, then?

Ron Yes. We shouldn't be long, only an hour or so.

Deryn Great.

Ron (*making for the hall*) Well I'll just have a quick wash, Simon, and I'm ready.

Deryn I think Simon's mother is in the bathroom.

Ron Is she?

Deryn Well, I heard someone in there after I'd come out.

Ron Oh well I'll just have a quick wash in the kitchen then. Won't be a tick.

Ron goes

Deryn He's just like you told me.

Simon moves up the settee and makes room for Deryn

Simon What about my mother?

Deryn Oh she's just like you told me, too.

Simon I was hoping I'd be wrong. I thought at one point on the journey down that you might be saying to me "What's all this rubbish about your mother, she's lovely". But she's not. She's exactly as I knew she would be.

Deryn I still think it was a mistake to bring me.

Simon No. She'd have to see you. Bringing you here is the only way I can hope she won't come visiting us after she's told.

Deryn When are you going to tell her?

Simon Sometime tonight.

Deryn She's not going to take it the way your father did.

Simon Don't I know it.

Deryn He's not like your mother at all, is he?

Simon No, thank God!

Deryn He's so nice. Homely.

Simon He makes up for her, I suppose.

Deryn He'd be like that, anyway.

Simon Yes. I don't understand my mother, I really don't. I've tried, but it isn't any use. (*He gets up and goes to the window*) She's like a plastic bag without any holes. She'd suffocate me if I'd let her. She desperately needs to love me, and the more she tries the more she pushes me away. I can see it, my father can, but not her. I wonder why.

Deryn Perhaps she's not aware of it?

Simon Oh, she is. He's told her. He's told me he's told her. The annoying thing is I know how she feels, what she's going through, even though I don't understand it, and I can't help her. If I show her any compassion whatsoever she'd strangle me. And all in the name of love.

Deryn I'll never love you like that.

They kiss

Ron comes in from the kitchen. He sees them and clears his throat

Ron Ready when you are.
Simon You're sure you won't come?
Deryn Positive.
Simon Right, well we'll see you in an hour then.

Simon and Ron go out into the hall

Deryn watches them leave from the window. After the car is heard starting up and pulling away Deryn takes a book from the small table and comes to sit on the settee

After a few seconds Iris comes into the room. She has a large envelope which she puts down on the small half-moon table. She is upset. She crosses behind the settee on her way to the kitchen

Deryn hears Iris sniffle

Deryn Oh, it's you. I didn't hear you come in.

Iris looks at her, she has obviously been crying

Is there anything wrong?
Iris Why should it interest you?
Deryn There isn't any need for you to be like this, you know.
Iris Like what?
Deryn Like you are.
Iris I didn't realize there was anything wrong with me.
Deryn You've been upset.
Iris What if I have.
Deryn It's Simon, isn't it?

She doesn't answer

Me, then.
Iris Yes.
Deryn I've done something to upset you?
Iris It's filth and I won't have filth in my house.
Deryn What are you talking about?
Iris There's no other word for it, it's just plain filth.
Deryn I don't understand.
Iris This is what I'm talking about. (*She shows Deryn the large brown envelope*) These filthy drawings.
Deryn (*standing*) You've been in my room.
Iris They're disgusting.
Deryn What right do you have to search my room?
Iris When you told me you drew people you forgot to mention you drew them naked.
Deryn What kind of a woman are you? Don't you have any respect for people's privacy? It's no wonder Simon never wants to come home.
Iris That's right, change the subject to Simon.
Deryn I'm not changing the subject.
Iris Yes you are. But let me tell you this. I know my son, I know him better

than you do, and when he finds out that you keep drawings of naked men——
Deryn When he finds out?
Iris Yes. He'll drop you like a hot——
Deryn Don't you think he already knows?
Iris No, I don't. How could he?
Deryn (*after a slight pause*) I think you'd better take another look at those sketches, and pay more attention to the face this time.
Iris (*a little taken back*) You're not going to try and tell me that it's Simon you've drawn.
Deryn I don't have to tell you anything. All you have to do is take another look and see for yourself.

Iris is almost tempted, but then pushes the envelope at Deryn which she takes

Iris No. Simon wouldn't involve himself in filth like that.
Deryn It's not filth, it's art.
Iris (*crossing to* R *behind the settee*) Oh, I might have known you'd call it that.
Deryn It is art. It's beautiful. You said yourself he's beautiful, or was it pretty? I can't remember.
Iris (*standing upstage of the armchair*) You could have drawn anyone. You could have drawn anyone and put Simon's face in afterwards.
Deryn I could have, yes, but I didn't.
Iris I don't believe you.
Deryn Ask Simon then; I'm sure he'll tell you.
Iris I don't believe it is Simon.
Deryn Then take another look. If you look close enough you'll see I've drawn his birthmark. A small strawberry about two inches from his navel?

This is the last straw for Iris. She snatches the envelope from Deryn and tears it open. She scrutinizes one of the sketches. After seeing Simon's likeness she fails to hold back her emotion. She sits in the armchair

Well?
Iris Get out.
Deryn Do you believe me now?
Iris (*raising her voice*) Get out! Get out!
Deryn It's your own fault. You had no right in my room.
Iris (*shouting*) I want you out of my house!
Deryn Are you sure about that?
Iris I want you out! I want you to leave me alone!

Deryn looks at Iris for a moment then goes out of the room

Iris, still very much upset, tears up the sketches as——

—the CURTAIN *falls*

ACT II

SCENE 1

The same. One hour later

When the CURTAIN *rises there is no-one on stage*

A car is heard stopping in the drive. Car doors are heard slamming and the doorbell chimes. It chimes again

Ron comes to the window and peers into the room

Ron There can't be anyone in.
Simon (*off*) Deryn wouldn't be far.
Ron I'll go round the back.

Ron goes round to the back of the house and Simon gives the doorbell another try. Ron eventually comes in from the kitchen and goes straight out into the hall. Simon enters carrying two conifers. Not sure where to put them, he hovers at the left of the settee. Ron comes in carrying two other plants

Out to the kitchen with them quick. She'll be off her head if she sees us in here with these.

They go out to the kitchen. After they have left the room Iris comes in from upstairs. Just as she is about to sit on the settee Simon enters

Simon There you are. We couldn't get an answer. Dad had to go round the back.
Iris I went for a lie down. I must have dropped off.
Simon Seen Deryn anywhere?
Iris (*after a slight pause*) She was in here the last time I saw her.
Simon Perhaps she's in the garden; she said she might be. She wanted to do some sketches of the house.
Iris Oh, so she does still life as well, does she?
Simon Deryn can do anything.

Ron comes in from the kitchen carrying a conifer

Ron Do you think this one looks a bit——(*He sees Iris*) Oh heck!

Iris opens her mouth to tell him not to bring in the conifer, but before she can say a word he has turned on the spot and is already on his way to the kitchen

Ron exits

Simon We had two smashing conifers for the front lawn.

Iris How nice!

Simon We were going to get you a rhododendron bush but we couldn't get it in the car.

Iris Don't they deliver?

Simon We didn't think of that.

Iris That's typical of your father that is, typical. That's the trouble with him, he never thinks.

Simon I was there too.

Iris Yes. You're just as bad as he is. But you're young, you'll learn.

Simon I'm twenty-three.

Iris I know how old you are. (*She looks at him for a moment*) Your hair's getting long.

Simon Perhaps it's because it hasn't been cut.

Iris Are you being sarcastic?

Simon No, just stating the obvious.

Iris It is on the long side.

Simon I'm leaving it to grow.

Iris What for?

Simon For no reason. I just don't fancy getting it cut.

Iris There's a new hairdressing shop opened up on Queen Street.

Simon (*not really interested*) Is there?

Iris Yes, Uni— (*she almost says the word sex*) something or other. It does them both, boys and girls.

Simon Deryn will cut mine when I'm ready.

Iris You didn't tell me she was a hairdresser as well.

Simon She's not.

Iris And you're going to let her cut your hair?

Simon She cuts her own.

Iris Need I say more?

Simon (*snapping*) There's nothing wrong with Deryn's hair.

Iris Did I say there was?

Simon You implied as much.

Iris If the cap fits ...

Simon Look, Mum. (*He ponders for a moment*) Oh, never mind.

Iris Have you something to say to me, Simon?

Simon pauses

Simon (*shaking his head*) It'll keep. (*He wanders over to the window*)

Iris No, I want to know now. If there's something I ought to know, I want to know now.

Simon It looks like rain.

Iris Don't change the subject, tell me.

Simon Tell you what?

Iris (*going to Simon at the window*) Whatever it was you were going to tell me just now.

Simon I don't want to argue with you.

Iris Who said we're arguing?

Simon Me, I said it.

Iris Don't be silly.
Simon I'm not being anything.
Iris You're being devious.
Simon No, I'm not.
Iris Tell me what's on your mind, then?

Simon doesn't answer. He moves slightly L

It's got something to do with her, hasn't it?
Simon Do you mean Deryn?
Iris You know perfectly well who I'm talking about.
Simon Even dogs have names.
Iris I'll find out. Whatever it is; I'll find out.
Simon I knew you'd be like this.
Iris I said yesterday. I told your father yesterday that there was something.
Simon (*moving slightly* R) I knew you'd take an instant dislike to her no matter what she was like.
Iris And if I'm not mistaken he knows all about it.
Simon If I'd brought a mate home though, that would have been a different story.
Iris I've never chosen your friends.
Simon Only because I'd never let you.
Iris That's not true.
Simon But it is.
Iris You've always brought home who you liked.
Simon What about Peter Harvey then?

Iris looks away

Do you remember the fuss you made about him?
Iris (*crossing* R *and sitting in the armchair*) I didn't like you mixing with boys of that sort.
Simon Boys of what sort?
Iris You know what I mean.
Simon He was my friend. Just because he lived in a council house he wasn't allowed over our doorstep.
Iris There were other reasons too.
Simon Rubbish. You were a snob. You were a snob then and you still are now.
Iris (*almost crying*) How dare you!
Simon You're not real.
Iris Oh, so she's got you saying it now, has she?
Simon Saying what?
Iris (*crying again*) She called me that last night. She said I wasn't real last night.
Simon (*after a slight pause*) Look, don't get upset.
Iris I don't have to put up with that, you know. And I'm not putting up with it, not from her or you either.
Simon (*frustrated*) I'm sorry.
Iris I'm your mother, remember that.

Simon (*moving in front of the settee*) It's you who should remember that, not me.
Iris What do you mean by that?
Simon What I say.
Iris Explain what you mean.
Simon We always seem to argue. All the time we argue. Why can't you be like any other mother?
Iris Tell me, go on. Tell me what you meant when you said it's I should remember that I'm your mother.
Simon (*sitting on the settee*) It's difficult to explain.
Iris Well try.
Simon I don't want to hurt you.
Iris I don't see why not, you do it all the time.
Simon If I do it's because you make me.
Iris I've never been able to make you do anything in your life.
Simon That's not true. You know that's not true. For years everything had to be your way.

They look at each other

Everything. Until one day I realized I had a mind and a will of my own.
Iris You still haven't answered my question.
Simon You've never really been able to accept that, have you?
Iris Accept what?
Simon That I have a life of my own. I know it's killing you, or killing us, but it's my life, Mum, and you've got to let me live it.
Iris I've never interfered.
Simon Never interfered? You'd even do my thinking for me if I'd let you.
Iris There was a time when I had to.
Simon Yes, when I was young. When I was a child. But I'm not your child any more.
Iris Oh, yes, you are.
Simon All right, all right, I am your child, but I'm not a child. I'm over twenty-one.
Iris Age doesn't make men.
Simon Maybe not, but mothers like you don't, either.

At this remark Iris takes a hanky from her sleeve and cries into it as she goes back up to the window

Iris (*quietly*) All I ever wanted to do was to love you.
Simon But you used that love like a gun.
Iris Only to protect you.
Simon But it can kill me, too. Don't you think I want you to love me?
Iris I do love you.
Simon In the way that other sons are loved?
Iris I don't know how other sons are loved. I don't care. All I've ever cared about is you.
Simon You can love someone too much, you know.
Iris And you think I've done that with you?

Simon I know you have.

Iris It's not fair, it's not fair that I should be blamed for that.

Simon Well it's not my fault.

Iris No, I know, I know. (*She stares at him for a moment, tears in her eyes*) They told me I would never have children. There was something wrong, I don't remember what. Your father and I were married nine years before you came along. Nine years. I couldn't believe it when they told me. A miracle they said. But I wanted you so much. I prayed every night, never missed, I still do. One day you'll want something very much, and perhaps then you'll know what it's like. Perhaps, then, we'll see how detached you can be.

Simon No-one's asking you to be detached.

Iris (*moving behind the settee*) What are you asking me to be, then? What do you want me to do? Love you from a distance? I can't do that, Simon, I can't. It would be easier for me to hate you first.

Simon All I want is for you to accept me as an adult. Speak to me as if I were one.

Iris If you were to act like one Simon, then, maybe I would.

Simon (*raising his voice*) That's not fair. I'm not acting like a child. If anyone's doing that, it's you.

Iris (*shouting*) Me?

Simon Look, we're arguing again. It's always the same, isn't it? I'm never home long before it starts.

Iris Just remember I'm your mother. I always have been and I always will be. If I'm still alive when you're fifty, you'll still be my boy.

Simon (*moving DL*) But why? Why won't you let go?

Iris Because you're my son. And I'll fight all the way for you. She thinks she's going to win you but she's not.

Simon Who, Deryn?

Iris I'll fight her to the end.

Simon But you're fighting the wrong one. It's not Deryn you have to contend with, it's me.

Iris I can't fight you.

Simon Mum, you've been fighting me for years. You used to win, too, so easily, but not anymore. I've got better at it. Each time you fought me it got more and more difficult for you to win. Believe me, if there's anything left worth saving, and I think there is, don't fight me. Don't fight me because if you do, this time you'll lose. (*He pauses. He steps nearer to her*) Mum, please? I'm only home until Monday.

She looks at him with tears in her eyes, then she smiles and he does too

Ron comes in from the kitchen

Ron (*to Simon*) I thought you said Deryn was in the garden.

Iris breaks away and sits DR in the armchair

Simon Isn't she there?

Ron I can't find her anywhere.

Simon She shouldn't be far.
Ron Maybe she's gone for a walk.
Simon No, she wanted to sketch the house, remember? I wonder if she's in her room.

Iris looks sharply at Simon

Simon goes out to the hall

(*Off, calling*) Deryn? Deryn?
Ron You wouldn't have any idea where she is, would you?
Iris (*without looking at him*) She was in here the last time I saw her.

Simon comes back into the room

Simon Well, I don't think she's up there.
Ron I hope she hasn't forgotten about my sketch.
Simon Of course she hasn't.
Iris (*alarmed*) She's going to sketch you, Ron?
Ron Yes, apparently she's very good. (*He winks at Simon*)
Iris Who said?
Ron Simon.
Iris (*almost laughing*) Yes, well, he would, wouldn't he?

They all begin to laugh but in a way they all seem afraid to

Simon I'll go and have another look in the garden.
Ron She's not there.

Simon goes out through the kitchen

(*Stepping a little nearer Iris*) Was I dreaming or did the three of us almost share a joke together?
Iris Go on, we often laugh.

Ron goes up to the window

Simon and I often laugh together. It just so happens that you were in on it this time.
Ron (*looking out of the window*) He won't find her in the garden, she's not out there.
Iris Remind me to take that cream out of the freezer, will you, Ron?
Ron I've already done it. I took it out before I went to the nursery.
Iris There's a gateau there, too. I think we'll have that as well.
Ron (*still looking out of the window*) Iris?
Iris It's pineapple if I remember. Simon likes pineapple, or at least he used to.
Ron (*moving* L *of the settee*) Iris?
Iris But he's changed so much I don't know what his likes and dislikes are.
Ron (*raising his voice*) Iris?
Iris Yes?
Ron I'm going to ask you a question and I want the truth.
Iris I've never lied to you, Ron.

Ron (*after a slight pause*) Do you have any idea where Deryn can be?

Iris (*looking away*) I told you, she was in here the last time I saw her.

Ron That's no answer.

Iris What more do you want to know?

Ron Did something happen between you and Deryn while Simon and I were out?

Iris What makes you think that?

Ron I don't think it. Or at least I don't *think* I think it. (*Sitting on the right hand side of the settee*) It's just a possibility, that's all. And knowing how you've been to her since she arrived it's a very strong possibility.

Iris (*swallowing*) We had a row.

Ron I might have known.

Iris It wasn't my fault, Ron, honest. I thought it all over and decided to meet her half way, fifty-fifty, but then I found the sketches.

Ron What sketches?

Iris They were awful, Ron, awful. They upset me.

Ron You found sketches?

Iris Yes.

Ron Where?

Iris In her suitcase.

Ron You went looking in Deryn's suitcase?

Iris I had to, I had to, I don't know why. It just drew me to it like a magnet.

Ron You had no right to go into her room, Iris.

Iris It's my house.

Ron It's Deryn's room.

Iris But they were awful, Ron.

Ron You still had no right.

Iris So awful.

Ron Why? Why should you get upset about an awful sketch?

Iris There was more than one.

Ron All right, sketches then. Why were they so awful?

Iris They were of Simon.

Ron There's nothing awful about that.

Iris They were of Simon, naked.

Ron (*after a slight pause; beginning to laugh*) I see.

Iris Don't laugh. How dare you laugh!

Ron (*still laughing*) That's why they upset you.

Iris Stop laughing.

Ron Well, serve you right. You had no right to go in there in the first place.

Iris Can you imagine what it was like for me, Ron, when I opened the envelope and took those things out?

Ron Were they good?

Iris Oh, I thought you might ask that. That's typical of you, that is.

Ron Perhaps they weren't of Simon. Perhaps they were of someone else.

Iris It was Simon all right, I could tell at a glance.

Ron They must have been good then.

Iris She even drew his birthmark just to leave no doubt.

Ron Now what do you mean by that? I suppose you're convinced, now, are you, that Deryn left those sketches, tucked away in her suitcase on the top shelf of her wardrobe, just so you'd find them?

Iris Nothing would surprise me as far as that girl is concerned. (*She moves behind the settee*)

Ron (*after a slight pause*) You had a row, you said. Then what happened?

Iris I got angry. I got angry and told her to leave.

Ron Oh, no!

Iris I told her to get out of my house.

Ron And did she?

Iris Well it looks like, doesn't it?

Ron (*picking up a newspaper*) Well, you've done it this time, Iris.

Iris She riled me. I lost my temper.

Ron You'll have to tell Simon.

Iris That she's left?

Ron Yes.

Iris Perhaps she hasn't left. Perhaps she's just gone to cool off. God knows she needed to. You should have seen her, Ron, she was like a raving lunatic.

Ron Yes, well as I said, you had no right to go snooping.

Simon comes in from the kitchen

Simon Well, she's definitely not in the garden. I'll just make sure she's not lying down. Maybe she's dropped off or something.

Simon goes upstairs

Ron I hope she is sleeping, Iris, or you're in trouble.

Iris That's right; put the blame on me. I expect she has gone. That's what she wanted. She wanted to leave. That way she could turn Simon against me.

Ron Don't be ridiculous.

Iris Ridiculous is it? I'm telling you, Ron, it's all been planned. She planned all this before she came.

Ron Why should she do that?

Iris So that she could turn Simon against me.

Ron I can't see what she'd gain by doing that.

Iris (*going and sitting in the armchair*) Honestly, Ron, honestly, sometimes you're as daft as a ... (*She can't find the word*) She likes him. She wants him for herself.

Ron She wants to marry him, you mean?

Iris Of course she does.

Ron Well she doesn't have to turn Simon against you to do that, does she?

Simon rushes into the room

Simon (*coming* C) She's not there, nothing's there, it's all gone, even her suitcase.

Ron I think you'd better sit down, Simon.

Simon (*to Iris*) What's happened? Where is she?

Ron Iris. You'd better explain.

Simon Where's Deryn?

Iris Well, to be perfectly honest, I don't know.

Simon Something's happened.

Iris Yes, yes, you could say that, yes.

Simon Well tell me then!

Iris It all started when I found some filthy sketches. I was dusting her room and I found some filthy sketches.

Simon Where did you find them?

Iris In her suitcase.

Simon (*stepping closer to her*) Since when have you started dusting suit-cases?

Iris That's not the point.

Simon You went snooping in her room hoping to find something.

Iris And I did, much to my disappointment.

Simon Rubbish! You were hoping to find something like that. I suppose the filth you're talking about are the sketches of me?

Iris And I suppose you call it art?

Simon Of course it's art, they're beautiful. They're worth quite a bit, too. We've sold them. We brought them down to show you before they go. Some Americans are buying them for fifty pounds each. You don't have to tell me any more. I can figure the rest out for myself. Did she leave of her own accord, or did you tell her to go?

Iris There was a row. I might have told her to leave.

Ron (*cautiously*) Iris.

Iris Yes all right I did, I'm sure I did. I was angry, she was too. We both said a lot of things. I didn't mean her to leave.

Simon Why didn't you stop her then?

Iris I didn't know she'd gone. I was in the kitchen when I heard the front door slam.

Simon You could have gone after her.

Iris I did, but she'd gone. I couldn't see her anywhere. Almost disappeared into thin air.

Simon Well I hope you're satisfied.

Iris Sit down.

Simon You must be joking. (*Going to the door*) I'm going to find Deryn.

Iris (*standing*) No please, please, sit down. Ron, tell him to sit down.

Ron This is nothing to do with me.

Iris (*going to him*) Please, Simon?

Simon There's no point, I've nothing to say to you.

Iris I don't want you to say anything, I just want you to listen.

Simon (*turning to her*) I'm sick of listening to you. I don't want to hear your voice anymore, it makes me sick.

Iris (*hurt*) Don't say that.

Simon You do it every time, don't you? Everything I've ever wanted in my life you've rejected.

Iris No, don't say anymore, just listen, listen to me for two minutes, please? Is that too much to ask for, two minutes?

Simon sighs

Whether you believe me or not, all I've ever said or done, I've done with your interest at heart.

Simon turns away

I have, Simon, I have. If I've hurt you sometimes it's only because I had to. Believe me it used to hurt me far more.

Simon Liar. You get some kind of pleasure out of saying "no" to me. You must do, you do it so often.

Iris I've never hurt you deliberately. (*She pauses*) If she has gone ...

Simon Who?

Iris You know who I'm talking about.

Simon (*turning to her; shouting*) Don't you think it hurts to know you won't even say her name?

Iris If she has gone, surely it's her that's doing the hurting, not me.

Simon You told her to go, remember.

Iris Yes, and I'm sorry I did now, I played it straight into her hands.

Simon I'm sure Deryn didn't want to leave.

Iris (*moving* UR) She didn't want to come. Go on, deny it, deny that.

Simon OK! So she didn't want to come, but she didn't want to leave either.

Iris Well, she certainly didn't argue that point.

Simon Would you stay in someone's house if they had told you to leave?

She doesn't answer

No. Well if you've finished. I'm off.

Iris (*shouting*) No, I haven't finished. (*Going to him; more quietly this time*) Look, can't we forget it? Start all over again? Put it all down to a misunderstanding.

Simon You can't put my whole upbringing down to a misunderstanding.

Iris I'm not talking about your upbringing, I'm talking about this situation.

Simon Putting this situation right isn't going to solve anything. There's much more to it than that.

Iris Now you're making excuses.

Simon No I'm not, I'm stating facts.

Iris (*moving* C) I've offered to forget it all. What more can I do than that? I don't think you want to forget it, do you? If the truth were known.

Simon It's not that. Anyway I can't speak for Deryn. Maybe she's not prepared to forget it even if I am.

Iris (*shouting*) Not prepared? Listen to you and she's the only one who's been hard done by.

Simon She is.

Iris What about me, then? What about what I've been through?

Simon Whatever humiliation you've felt it was all self-inflicted.

Iris (*moving to the armchair*) Don't you think she humiliated me?

Simon I've told you, all your emotions are self-inflicted. Even your so called love for me.

Iris (*sitting in the armchair*) My love for you isn't an infliction.

Simon That's a matter of opinion.

Iris (*crying*) It's not.

Simon What is it, then?

She doesn't answer

I'll tell you what it is, it's an obsession. A disease. A cancer. And the
terrible thing is, it's not killing you, it's killing us. (*He steps closer to her*)
You want to love me in a way I won't let you, and I want you to love me
in a way that you can't. That's the long and the short of it, isn't it?

Iris (*still upset*) Can't we find a compromise?

Simon There isn't one. If there was I'm sure we would have found it a long
time ago. (*He pauses*) I think I'd better go now. (*He turns to leave*)

Iris Are you going to look for her?

Simon (*angrily*) Of course.

Iris (*raising her voice*) Why her? Why couldn't it have been someone else?

Simon It wouldn't have made any difference. Don't you see that? No matter
what girl I'd have brought home it would have been the same. Deryn
being Deryn hasn't anything to do with it. You just used her as an excuse.

Iris (*after a slight pause*) If you find her are you coming back?

Simon I don't know if Deryn will come back again.

Iris Does that mean you won't either?

Simon (*softly*) I don't know.

Iris (*bitterly*) She's only a girl. For her you'll give up your whole family?

Simon I don't have to give up everything for Deryn, but I will if I need to.
She may be only a girl to you, but she's more than that to me.

Iris (*more hurt than angry*) If you leave with her, Simon, you don't come
back.

Ron looks at her

Simon (*after a slight pause*) I don't think I want to come back again.

Iris Not even if you're in trouble, I don't want to know.

Simon I'd never turn to you if I was.

Iris (*hurt*) Wouldn't you?

Simon I never have. (*He looks at Ron*) If you think about it.

Iris Yes, you're right. It's always been him you've turned to.

Simon Because Dad would always help me without any questions. And
once it was over it was forgotten about.

Iris You've always had this thing between you.

Simon A bond.

Iris No, more than that. A barrier. A barrier that I could never break.

Simon I don't know why; you put it there.

Iris (*crying again*) I've always felt left out. Not really part of anything.

Simon That's because you're not capable of taking part. Not in a family
anyway. You take over. Suddenly it's not a threesome anymore, suddenly
it's you and us.

Iris (*with new found determination*) So that's how you feel, is it?

Simon That's how it is, how it's always been.

Iris (*raising her voice*) You've never complained about it before you met
her. Why has this started only since she's been on the scene?

Simon (*exploding*) Oh I give up, I really do. (*He makes for the door*) I'm
   going.
Iris Go on, you go to her, then. You go to her. But just you remember what
   I said. She's the type that will get you into trouble. Get herself pregnant or
   something. Just to make a good catch.
Simon She already is pregnant. And it's not Deryn who's going to get a
   good catch, it's me.

Simon goes

*Iris looks at Ron who looks up from his newspaper. He sees Iris's face and
quickly returns to the sports page*

Black-out

SCENE 2

The same. Later that evening

*The Lights come up on Ron who is sitting in the armchair smoking his pipe and
doing the crossword, and Iris, who is on the settee browsing through a
photograph album. After a few seconds Ron looks up in search for a word. His
eyes catch sight of Iris with the album and crying into her hanky*

Ron I wish you'd put that away, Iris.
Iris (*without looking up*) I wish you'd stop doing crosswords.
Ron You'd do better looking at the Highway Code than that, you know.
Iris How can I take my test now? How will I be able to concentrate now
   when my mind is full of other things.
Ron You are supposed to put everything out of your mind when you are
   driving.
Iris That's what I mean. That's why I've decided not to take my test.
Ron Don't be silly.
Iris Oh, I'm silly as well now, am I?
Ron As well as what?
Iris As well as everything else I'm supposed to be.
Ron Can't you leave it alone? It's gone now; forget about it.
Iris (*crying*) It's all right for you to say forget about it. That's easier said
   than done. It's one thing to be called silly, but it's completely different
   when you're told that—that—you're not real.

She cries again. Ron tuts and returns to his crossword

   That's right, go back to your crossword. Don't worry about me, I'll be all
   right. You'll be reading in there one day that I've done away with myself
   in the bathroom. Then perhaps you'll sit up and take a bit of notice. If for
   some reason though, Ron, you go before me, I won't cremate you like you
   want. I'll bury you just for spite.
Ron That's all right, I won't mind. Bury me if you want to. But, preferably

three down and four across. (*A slight pause in which he stares at Iris for a moment*) Are you serious about your test?

Iris I've never been more serious about anything in my life.

Ron Well, I hope you're not going to blame Simon and Deryn.

Iris Who else is to blame, then?

Ron No-one. It's no-one's fault.

Iris (*about to cry again*) I don't know how he could do it to me. He's had everything he's ever wanted.

Ron No, Iris, he's had everything you've wanted to give him. That's not quite the same thing.

Iris So what are you saying then? That he hasn't had all he wanted?

Ron No, he hasn't.

Iris (*after a slight pause*) I suppose you're referring to the time he wanted to keep a horse in the front garden, are you?

Ron All right then, yes, take that for an example.

Iris Have you ever heard of anything so ridiculous? Keeping a horse on the front lawn! (*She moves to the mirror*)

Ron He was only nine at the time, Iris. You should have explained to him, not carry on the way you did. If you had only taken the trouble to explain to him he'd have understood. But you couldn't do that, could you? Instead you had to make a huge fuss, bring it up every time it suited you, even years later, even now. He'd have forgotten all about it if you had let him. But you couldn't. By always bringing it up you constantly reminded him of the time you wouldn't let him have a horse. It sounds silly now and childish, and it is, but it's a prime example of what went wrong.

Iris With who?

Ron With you and Simon.

Iris There's nothing wrong with me, Ron, nothing. As for Simon you might be right. I think there is something wrong with him. I don't *think*—I *know*. It's that girl. She's a bad lot.

Ron You may as well know it now, Iris, I'll have nothing said about Deryn; she's a nice girl.

Iris So she's got you fooled as well, has she?

Ron (*standing up*) Oh give it up, will you? Just give it up.

Iris (*almost crying*) Yes, they can walk all over me and you just don't care, do you? You just don't care.

Ron (*going to her*) Of course I care. I've always cared. I wouldn't be here if I didn't care.

Iris (*turning to face him*) Is he going to come back, Ron?

Ron I don't know. I don't know what his plans are.

Iris I've got to see him again. I've got to, I've got to tell him things.

Ron I think you've probably told him too much already.

Iris (*finding the next line difficult to say*) Do you think he hates me?

Ron (*not sure how to answer*) I think he could love you a lot more.

Iris If I've hurt him it wasn't deliberate.

Ron He's afraid to love you.

Iris Afraid?

Ron I think he tried it once and didn't like it.

Iris (*putting her head on his chest*) What can I do? What can I do to make him love me?

Ron Nothing, love. You're too late. (*Holding her arm*) You can't make someone love you anyway. *You* ought to know that.

Iris (*pulling away*) What do you mean?

Ron Could you ever love Deryn?

She turns away

Do you know what I mean now?

Iris There must be something I can do. I can't just leave it with him walking out like that.

Ron (*going back to his chair*) Better for you if you did leave it. I think if he was to see you now it would (*not quite sure how to put it*) well, keep out of his way if I were you. Unless of course he wants to see you. It would be all right then. It would be all right then, because then it would be something that he'd want.

Iris (*moving behind the settee*) I've got to see him.

Ron (*sitting in the chair*) Take my advice for once, will you?

Iris He'll come back, I know he will.

Ron In time he might.

Iris No, tonight. He'll come back tonight, I know it.

Ron If he does it will only be to collect his things.

Iris (*going to the window*) I won't mind just as long as I see him.

Ron If you do you'll regret it.

Iris For two minutes, that's all, two minutes.

Ron It'll be fatal.

Iris I only want to tell him that . . .

Ron You're sorry?

Iris (*moving slightly towards him*) I forgive him.

Ron For what?

Iris For getting in trouble.

Ron Iris, in those two minutes you'll hang yourself seven times over. The boy doesn't believe he is in trouble.

Iris She's pregnant, isn't she?

Ron That's not his trouble, that's his joy. He's proud of it.

Iris It's nothing to be proud of.

Ron It's nothing to be ashamed of either.

Iris You'll be telling me that you're proud of him next.

Ron I am. I've always been proud of him.

Iris Even now?

Ron They love each other. He's not ashamed of it. Why should I be?

Iris (*moving to the settee*) Well I'll say this for you, you certainly stick together.

Ron Isn't that what it's all about?

Iris (*sitting on the settee*) I don't know how I'm going to hold my head up in this place again.

Ron You had a human being for a son, Iris, not a monk. I know it's been something of a blow for you but it's proved one thing at least, the boy's no different from anyone else. Take my advice and if he does come here tonight, stay out of his way.

Iris You don't know what you're asking.

Ron I know it's not going to be easy for you, but it would be best. Unless of course he wants to see you.

Iris He should want to.

Ron Why? You've upset him.

Iris What about me? Everybody's going on about Simon, what about me?

Ron I gather by "everybody" you mean me?

Iris I've been hurt, too.

Ron I think you've probably hurt him more.

Iris No, Ron, you're wrong. I know I'm me, and I can't help being what I am, but you can't say how hurt I've been. *You* can't measure my hurt against someone else's. No-one can.

Ron True, true. It's just that I understand more of how he feels. (*He puts his pipe on the arm of the chair*) How can I explain? (*He gets up and sits next to Iris on the settee*) Do you remember the first time I took you home to meet my parents?

Iris Remember it? I'll never forget it. It was in the middle of August, hot. Everything was going well until we sat at the table for tea. A cold meat salad. I remember. I didn't want it but I was too shy to say "no" in those days. I swear I don't know to this day if that tomato was soft or the knife blunt, but it wouldn't cut it. Instead it burst, and squirted right across the table up the front of your sister's dress and straight into her face; I almost died.

Ron (*smiling, trying to remember*) Was it Lilian or Rosemary?

Iris Lilian. I'm sure that's why she never bothers with us, you know. She's never really forgiven me for that hot day in August.

Ron I was proud of you.

Iris Even after that?

Ron I felt so big, so grown up.

Iris Well you should have. You were twenty-seven.

Ron You know what I mean. I'd taken you home for them to see you. For them to see what I'd found.

Iris You made me sound like a foreign coin.

Ron You must have felt something the same when you took me home?

Iris (*thinking about it*) I don't think I was proud.

Ron Charming.

Iris I don't know what it was I felt.

Ron I always thought I'd never made much of an impression on you, Iris. Now I'm convinced.

Iris I must have felt something, I suppose.

Ron It's too late to save my feelings.

Iris I just can't remember at the moment what it was.

Ron If I were you I'd forget about it. You never know, it might come back to you, later.

Iris Yes.

Ron You see my point though?

Iris What point?

Ron How I felt when I took you home. How Simon must have felt when he came home with Deryn.

Iris I didn't see it that way.

Ron But you do now? I mean it's too late to do anything about it. But it's something if you see and understand it now?

Iris pauses for a moment

Iris (*standing*) Do you remember that hat I bought myself for our silver wedding anniversary?

Ron looks at her

Do you remember how you took an instant dislike to it? Well that's exactly how I felt when she walked in here yesterday.

Ron That's not a fair comparison. I dislike all hats. Especially on you, you look so ridiculous.

Iris How dare you!

Ron Blue with silver bells, I ask you.

Iris It's a beautiful hat, Ron. I'd be wearing it now if you hadn't stopped me.

Ron I didn't stop you. You can wear the silly thing any time you want to. Just don't expect me to walk alongside you, that's all.

Iris That's what I mean!

Ron It's your own fault. You take everything too far. The hat's all right for wearing to church, to a wedding or a christening or something. But I draw the line when you put it on and expect me to walk with you to the butchers. How did we get on to the subject of your hat, anyway?

Iris I just wanted to point out that some people can have an instant dislike to something, or someone.

Ron (*standing*) You can't compare hats to people. (*He looks around the room*) Where's my pipe? (*He sees it on the arm of the chair*) Oh yes. (*He goes and sits in the chair*) Although I don't know, that hat of yours just about sums you up.

Iris Are you getting personal, Ron?

Ron (*taking a small pencil from his cardigan pocket and starting his crossword again*) Iris, I'm not getting anything.

Iris Are you trying to tell me something?

Ron Not really, no.

Iris What do you mean, "not really"? Either you are or you're not.

Ron No, I'm not, then.

Iris If you've got something on your mind, Ron, I think you ought to say it. (*She sits on the settee*)

Ron What's eight letters, begins with P, ends with C and——

Iris (*raising her voice*) Are you deliberately avoiding my question?

Ron Oh yes, platonic. (*He pretends to write in the word*)

Iris (*shouting*) Ron, I'm talking to you.

Ron If you don't mind me saying so, you'd hear a lot more if you didn't speak so much.

Iris And you'd speak a lot more if you'd listen to me.

Ron So what are you saying?

Iris I don't know. (*A slight pause*) I've forgotten what I was on about now.

Ron It was probably Deryn.

Iris No, it wasn't her. It was you, I think. (*She looks at him with her head cocked to one side*) Do you mind me talking about you, Ron?

Ron No. At least when you're talking about me you're giving someone else a rest.

Iris half opens her mouth to speak then realizes what he has said. She decides not to answer his last remark. She picks up the album again and looks through it. Suddenly she closes it and looks at Ron

Iris Tell me, Ron, and tell me the truth. Swear, swear on your mother's grave that you knew nothing of all this.

Ron Simon and Deryn you mean?

Iris Who else would I mean? Go on, Ron, go on, swear.

Ron takes his pipe out of his mouth and looks at her for a moment

Ron Bugger.

Iris I suppose that's your idea of a joke?

Ron I knew you wouldn't laugh. There's more humour in a bowl of cornflakes.

Iris (*shouting*) Answer me.

Ron What exactly did you want to know?

Iris If Simon confided in you.

Ron (*after a slight pause*) Do you believe me to be a man of my word, Iris?

Iris Yes.

Ron Well, there you are then, I am. (*He puts his pipe back into his mouth and returns to his crossword*)

Iris (*after thinking for a moment*) I don't quite follow you, Ron.

Ron You're not asking me to break a confidence, are you?

Iris Ah, so he did then.

Ron I didn't say that.

Iris You as good as.

Ron No I didn't.

Iris I knew it. He told you on the phone on Thursday night, didn't he?

Ron I swear to you that Simon never once mentioned to me on the phone on Thursday that Deryn was pregnant.

Iris (*a thought strikes her*) Perhaps she's not then. Perhaps he just said that in a moment of temper.

Ron No, I don't think so.

Iris Why?

Ron I just don't.

Iris Tell me why then? I'll tell you why, because you've already been told, haven't you? Haven't you?

Ron I'm his father, Iris. It was easier for him to tell me.

Iris (*getting up and moving downstage*) I knew it. And to think all day Friday you denied it.

Ron He didn't tell me on Friday.

Iris It's no wonder she didn't want to come.

Ron No, Iris. Deryn didn't want to come because, well because Simon had probably told her what you'd be like.

Iris It's terrible to think he talks about his mother like that.

Ron It's terrible to think he has to.

Iris I hope he's not thinking about doing the decent thing and marrying her, is he, Ron?

Ron I don't know.

Iris (*scornfully*) Ronald?

Ron (*raising his voice*) I don't know.

Iris He'd be a fool to throw it all away now with only two years to go.

Ron I'm sure he won't.

Iris What makes you so sure?

Ron He's not a fool. I've told you that before.

Iris If she was any sort of a girl she wouldn't let him anyway. I expect she told him she was on the pill.

He looks at her

That's how all this happened. Made him think he was on a safe thing, just to make a catch.

Ron I don't suppose you've thought of the possibility of them loving each other?

Iris It's a college romance. It will be over in three terms. He'll be in his final year and waiting the divorce the same time. And that's bound to affect his studying. Imagine sitting your final exam when your mind is full of divorce proceedings. He's bound to fail it now, Ron, he's bound to.

Ron Here you are, jumping the gun again. You're talking about divorce and they're not even married yet.

Iris If I know that girl half as well as I think I know her, it's all been planned.

Ron But you don't know her, do you? You only met her for the first time yesterday.

Iris I had her summed up the minute she set foot in this room. It's instinct, Ron. There's a lot to be said for woman's instinct.

Ron Perhaps they don't plan to marry. Perhaps they're going to live together.

Iris No, I don't think she'd settle for that. It's marriage or nothing for her. She wants to catch him, hook, line and sinker. (*A thought strikes her*) Unless they've told you different, have they?

Ron I haven't been told anything.

Iris You were told she was pregnant.

Ron I mean about their wedding, or them living together.

Iris I reckon if he told you about her being in the family way he's told you what his plans are, too.

Ron You're wrong, Iris.

Iris I'd like it proved.

Ron (*shouting*) I don't have to prove it. I'm telling you the truth.

Iris stares at him for a moment then goes back to the photo album. There is a long pause in which Ron looks out front and puffs his pipe

I bumped into Jack and Mary today.
Iris (*not really interested*) Oh, so they're back then.
Ron Flew home Wednesday.
Iris Funny day to fly home.
Ron Yes.
Iris (*without looking up from the album*) Where was it they went to?
Ron Venice.
Iris Oh yes, of course. I remember you saying now before they went.
Ron Saying what?
Iris (*looking at him*) That they went to Venice.

Ron continues to smoke his pipe and Iris looks back at the album

Ron (*after a slight pause*) I wouldn't mind going there myself.
Iris Your Lilian has lost weight since this was taken.
Ron I can't see you in a gondola though somehow.
Iris That Weight Watchers must be doing her good.
Ron Or do you fancy Naples?
Iris (*looking at him*) Pardon?
Ron Naples.
Iris What about it?
Ron Would you like to go there?
Iris What for?
Ron For a holiday, what do you think?
Iris (*thinking about it*) Naples?
Ron You could do with a holiday.
Iris I thought we were going to Cornwall.
Ron We can change our minds, we haven't booked.
Iris Why Naples?
Ron Well I don't know. It sounds nice.
Iris So does Rubella but I wouldn't like to catch it. You don't go to a place just because it sounds nice.
Ron Somewhere else then, go on. You name it and we'll go.

She doesn't answer

I know, Scotland. (*He joins her on the settee*) We might be able to get into the same hotel, the same room even. Come on, what do you think? Shall we? We'll treat it as a second honeymoon. We'll do everything the way we did it before, even down to the champagne in bed. Come on, shall we?
Iris (*after a pause; looking at him*) I had my heart set on Cornwall. Why this urge to take me on holiday all of a sudden?
Ron Well it would be a change, a rest for you.
Iris Well I could do with one, I will say that.
Ron Let's go then.
Iris (*unsure*) When?
Ron Anytime you like. Tomorrow, next week; now, if you like.

Iris Oh I couldn't think of going this month.

Ron Why not?

Iris I need at least four weeks to get over all this lot.

Ron (*standing and walking* DL) But that's the whole point of taking you away.

Iris Is it? So that's your little scheme, is it?

Ron It would be good for you, Iris. Gets you thinking about other things.

Iris You don't think that being in Cornwall or Naples is going to stop me thinking about Simon, do you?

Ron It's not healthy.

Iris It would be even worse then, not being on the telephone.

Ron You would be in Cornwall.

Iris But not in Naples.

Ron Of course you would, they've got telephones there too.

Iris Look, Ron, he doesn't ring me now he's two hundred miles away. I'm sure he's not going to pick up the phone and ring across the Atlantic.

Ron Atlantic?

Iris (*crying*) And if he did you could bet your life it would be on a Thursday.

Ron So you won't go then?

Iris I can't even think about it yet. Not for at least a month or two.

Ron (*walking towards the hall*) Oh well I tried.

Iris Where are you going?

Ron I think I'll go for a walk. Coming?

Iris At this time?

Ron It's not late.

Iris (*looking at her watch*) It's ten to nine.

Ron (*looking out of the window*) It's a lovely night.

Iris Will you be long?

Ron Come with me.

Iris I can't.

Ron Why not, ten minutes we'll be.

Iris I'm going to wash my hair.

Ron (*moving* C) You washed it this morning.

Iris There are a few dishes need washing——

Ron I've already done them.

Iris You go, go on, I'll be all right.

Ron (*after a slight pause*) He's not going to come, Iris.

Iris (*almost crying*) Yes he is, I know he is, and if I go with you he might come while we're out.

Ron Better for you if he does.

Iris Don't let's go over all that again.

Ron sits down in his chair

Well I'm not stopping you.

Ron I wanted us both to go.

Iris Only to get me out.

Ron It is a lovely night. A walk would have been nice.

Iris If you want to walk, buy a dog.

Ron That's not a bad idea.
Iris I wasn't serious.
Ron A dog would be nice. Company for us.
Iris I'm not having any dogs in this house.
Ron A cat then?

She turns her head away from him

A budgie?

The doorbell chimes. Iris looks quickly at Ron

I'll get it.

Ron goes out into the hall

Iris stands nervously. She goes to the mirror and pats her hair, then walks up to the window and peers out. Not able to see anything she turns back into the room. She goes to the hall door and listens at it, then walks over to the armchair

Ron comes back in

Iris (*sotto voce*) Is it him?
Ron (*sotto voce*) Come back for his things.
Iris Is he going to see me?
Ron (*coming downstage*) I haven't asked.
Iris (*taking one step nearer him*) Well, what did he say?
Ron Nothing.
Iris You were there all that time whispering nothing?
Ron What do you expect him to say?
Iris I don't know. I heard you whispering, that's all.
Ron He asked where you were.
Iris (*stepping a little closer*) Did he?
Ron Don't expect anything.
Iris (*a little closer*) Did he really ask?
Ron Only to avoid you, I think.
Iris (*hurt*) I see. (*She turns and walks away*) Where's the car? I didn't hear the car.
Ron He didn't bring it up the drive.
Iris Is she with him?
Ron No.
Iris Didn't he find her?
Ron Deryn's in the car. (*Going to her*) Don't go to him, Iris. Whatever you do, don't *you* go to him.

Ron looks at her for a moment then goes into the kitchen

Iris sits in the armchair with her back to the hall door

*After some time, Simon comes into the room. He closes the door and walks
L. He looks at Iris then looks away*

Suddenly, she becomes aware that he is in the room. She turns, sees him and stands. She is crying. She rushes to him

Iris (*through her tears*) I knew you'd come back, I knew you would. (*She embraces him*) Come and sit down. Move the album.

He picks it up and gives it to her. She puts it on the floor at the side of the settee. Simon sits down

We've been looking at photographs, reminiscing. Trying to take my mind off, well, you know. It didn't work though. I couldn't get you out of my mind.

Simon What about Deryn?

Iris (*reluctantly*) Yes, her too.

There is a pause. They both speak together

Simon } (*together*) { I think perhaps I . . .
Iris } (*together*) { If you want to ask . . .

Simon Sorry, go on.

Iris No you.

Simon (*standing*) I was going to say perhaps I shouldn't stay too long. Deryn is in the car.

Iris I was going to say if you want to ask her in . . .

Simon No, she won't.

Iris Ask her.

Simon I already have.

Iris I see. You're not staying then?

Simon Well I can't, can I?

Iris She'll stay if you ask her to. She told me on Friday, in this very room, that she couldn't say no to you. Practically finds it impossible, those were her words, ask her if you don't believe me.

Simon I don't want to ask her. I don't want to stay myself.

Iris But I thought that everything was all right now. I thought because you came to see me that everything was all right.

Simon Look, I can't say anymore. Everything has been said.

Ron comes in from the kitchen with a glass of water and two tablets. He puts them down on the small table and sits in the armchair

If I say it all again it would only be rubbing it in, and I don't want to do that.

Iris Aren't we going to talk about it?

Simon No.

Iris But why?

Simon Because you think you're right and I know you're not. To talk would mean to row or argue and I don't want to do either.

Iris But there's so much to be explained.

Simon I don't have any explaining to do.

Iris What about this baby?

Simon I don't have to explain that.

Iris I think I should have been told.

Simon You were going to be. I didn't want to tell you in the way that I did. It just happened that way. I'm sorry for that.

Iris How much is she?

Simon About twelve weeks I think.

Iris (*standing and going to him*) There's no doubt is there?

Simon What do you mean?

Iris She hasn't told you this so that, well, you know ...

Simon (*raising his voice*) We don't lie to each other.

Iris You're sure this is what you want?

Simon Yes.

Iris It's not too late to change your mind. Things can be arranged. Don't think of the expense, I'll see to all that.

Simon What are you suggesting?

Iris Well if for some reason you're not sure ...

Simon I am.

Iris If you want to change your mind.

Simon (*moving away*) I don't.

Iris (*turning to face him*) You don't have to do the decent thing. (*Going to him*) What I mean is, you're both very young.

Simon I love her.

Iris If she goes through with it, it could ruin both your lives.

Simon We love each other.

Iris You've got college and she's got whatever it is she does.

Simon She paints, remember?

Iris Well there you are, then. Reconsider, Simon, please?

Simon I won't change my mind.

Iris (*turning slightly away from him*) I can't help feeling that you're determined to go through with all this just to defy me.

Simon I'm not. Believe me I'm not.

Iris (*turning to face him again*) If she's only twelve weeks it's not too late.

Simon For what?

Iris Termination.

Simon Have an abortion, you mean?

Iris (*moving closer to him*) To have it terminated, yes.

Simon (*shouting*) It means the same thing. Do you know what you're suggesting?

Iris It would be for the best.

Simon You're asking me to destroy my child.

Iris It's not a child, not yet.

Simon You've destroyed your own and now you're asking me to do the same.

Iris I haven't destroyed you.

Simon You just did, what little was left.

Iris Can't you see I'm only suggesting it for your own good?

Simon How do you know what's good for me?

Iris Think of your career. If you have this child it would ruin it all.

Simon The baby's there. It's mine, and there's nothing going to stop me from doing what I want for once.

Iris (*moving away*) Well, if you're that determined.
Simon I am.
Iris Can I ask just one thing of you?
Simon No.
Iris Please, it's not too much to ask.
Simon (*after a pause*) What is it?
Iris (*going to him*) Don't marry her.
Simon (*shouting*) Not much to ask?
Iris It will be a mistake.
Simon You call asking me not to marry the girl I'm in love with not much to ask?
Iris I swear I won't ask you to do anything else.
Simon You're too late, we were married over a week ago.

There is a pause

Iris That's not true. You're lying. Tell me you're lying. You are, aren't you?

Simon Why should I lie?
Iris (*crying*) Oh God. (*She sits down on the settee crying*)

Simon turns upstage to the window

Simon (*with his back to the audience*) I think I could have forgiven you anything. Everything you've ever done to me. But when you suggested the destroying of my child that was the end as far as I'm concerned.

Simon turns to face her. She is crying helplessly

Don't ever come and visit us. I'm afraid you won't be welcome. As for the baby, he's not even going to know you exist. (*He steps a little nearer*) And should you decide to turn up one day, no matter when, I'll tell him who you are, and what your suggestion was to me when you heard of his conception.
Iris You're determined to hurt me, aren't you?
Simon I didn't come here for that.
Iris What did you come here for then?
Simon To collect my things.
Iris You didn't have to come in and see me.
Simon But I did. I want the sketches. You do have them, Deryn said she left them with you.
Iris (*still crying*) I—I destroyed them. I was angry. I didn't mean to.
Simon You destroyed all of them?
Iris I didn't realize they were of any value. I'm sorry, honestly. I'm sorry. I'm sorry, I'm sorry, I'm sorry.
Simon (*after a slight pause; turning to Ron*) Well I'm off now, Dad.
Ron (*standing and shaking Simon's hand*) Take care.
Iris I'm sorry.
Simon And you.
Ron Remember what I told you. (*He gestures money*)
Simon I will.

Simon turns and goes out of the door

Iris follows him but not out of the room. The front door slams. Iris goes to the window where she watches and cries

Ron Iris?

She doesn't answer

Iris?

She just cries

Shall I make something to drink?

She shakes her head

Have a cup of tea?

No reply

Coffee?

She doesn't answer

Complan then?

Iris No, nothing. I don't want anything.

Ron Do you want to talk about it? It'll be better if you talk.

Iris What's the point? (*She turns to him*) You never see anything my way, not where Simon is concerned. It's not fair. You've gone through it all without a scratch, and look at me, after all I've done. Brought him up on my own virtually.

Ron If you don't mind me saying so——

Iris I do. I know exactly what you're going to say and I do mind.

Ron (*going to her*) I warned you.

Iris (*raising her voice*) I said I mind.

Ron Well I'm going to tell you, anyway. Not that it's going to make a blind bit of difference, is it?

Iris So why waste your breath then?

Ron Because maybe once, just this once, you'll listen to me.

Iris I've heard it all before.

Ron But you've never listened.

Iris I only wanted him to have the best.

Ron Even the best wouldn't have been good enough for you.

Iris What's wrong with that?

Ron Nothing. Nothing at all. I don't think it's what you've given him that's been the problem. I think it's the way you gave it, and the reason why.

Iris That's me, I can't alter that.

Ron (*turning away*) No-one's asking you to undergo a major personality change. All that Simon ever asked for——

Iris He got.

Ron (*turning towards her again*) All Simon ever asked for was understanding, support sometimes in the things he felt important even if we thought they weren't.

Iris And you gave him all those things, I suppose?

Ron Yes, Iris, I did.

Iris Well, there we are then. If he had all that from you what more did he want.

Ron He didn't want any more. He didn't want it all from me, that's all. You should have done your bit, too, you know.

Iris Don't you think I did? Don't you think I encouraged him?

Ron Not in the things he needed encouragement in. I'm not sure if encouragement is the right word, or if it is, I don't know if it's that you should have given him. All I know is he never needed your . . .

Iris (*still very much upset*) Go on, say it. Tell me he never needed my love either.

Ron I wasn't going to say that. What I'm trying to say is, that whatever it was he wanted, needed, or decided to do, you would always deter him before he could do anything else. You must have realized.

Iris My only child and he does this to me.

Ron (*raising his voice*) He hasn't done anything to anybody.

Iris See what I mean? Nothing's ever Simon's fault, not ever.

Ron After all that's happened, and you still can't see it. (*He sighs*) I'm going to bed. Are you coming?

Iris (*up at the window looking out*) No.

Ron I'm going up then. (*He crosses and goes to the door. Before leaving the room; turning*) Your tablets are on the table.

Ron goes

Iris looks at the window crying, her back to the audience. The Lights fade leaving only the night light coming in from the window

CURTAIN

FURNITURE AND PROPERTY LIST

ACT I

SCENE 1

On stage: Settee. *On it:* two cushions, chairbacks, small ashtray on R arm
Armchair. *On it:* chairback; ashtray and newspaper on L arm
Bureau
Small table. *On it:* ashtray
Half-moon table. *On it:* a few books, large framed photograph of Simon
   aged six or seven
Waste-bin
Small cabinet. *On it:* vase containing three or four pampas grass
Pictures (preferably including a Constable) on walls
Gold-coloured, chunky-looking mirror hanging on UL wall

Personal: **Iris:** wrist-watch, hanky (used throughout)
Ron: pipe and matches, small pencil (used throughout)

ACT I

SCENE 2

Set: Cup of tea for **Iris**

Off stage: Tea plates, teacloth **(Ron)**
Large brown envelope containing two or three sketches **(Iris)**

ACT II

SCENE 1

On stage: As before

Off stage: Two small conifer trees **(Simon)**
Two plants **(Ron)**
Small conifer tree **(Ron)**

ACT II

SCENE 2

Set: Photograph album on settee for **Iris**

Off stage: Glass of water, two tablets **(Ron)**

LIGHTING PLOT

Practical fittings required: two wall lamps either side of bow window

Interior. A living-room. The same scene throughout

ACT I, SCENE 1. Late afternoon

To open: General effect of late afternoon light through window

Cue 1   **Iris** goes to the kitchen with **Ron** following behind sheepishly   (Page 16)
            Fade to black-out

ACT I, SCENE 2. Early afternoon

To open: General effect of afternoon light through window

No cues

ACT II, SCENE 1. Early afternoon

To open: General effect of afternoon light through window

Cue 2   **Ron** sees Iris's face and quickly returns to the sports page   (Page 39)
            Black-out

ACT II, SCENE 2. Mid-evening

To open: General effect of mid-evening light through window; practicals and
            covering spots on

Cue 3   **Ron:** "Your tablets are on the table."   (Page 53)
            *Start very slow interior fade, including practicals and covering
            spots*

EFFECTS PLOT

ACT I

Cue 1   **Iris:** "Well, he's still my boy and always will be."   (Page 5)
Telephone rings

Cue 2   **Iris:** "I think you're doing too many of them crosswords, Ron."   (Page 6)
Car driving up and stopping; car horn

Cue 3   **Iris:** "I said there's nothing."   (Page 6)
Two car doors slam; short pause, then doorbell chimes

Cue 4   **Iris:** "Well, you thought wrong, didn't you?"   (Page 6)
Doorbell chimes

Cue 5   **Iris:** "I wasn't going to have Simon blame me if she went."   (Page 17)
Doorbell chimes

Cue 6   **Ron:** ". . . going on about this coq-au-vin thing."   (Page 19)
Doorbell chimes

Cue 7   **Deryn** watches them leave from the window   (Page 26)
Car starting up and driving off

ACT II

Cue 8   To open   (Page 28)
Car stopping; three car doors slam; doorbell chimes, and then chimes again

Cue 9   **Ron:** "I'll go round the back."   (Page 28)
Doorbell

Cue 10   **Ron:** "A budgie."   (Page 48)
Doorbell chimes

Cue 11   **Iris** follows **Simon**   (Page 51)
Front door slams

MADE AND PRINTED IN GREAT BRITAIN BY
LATIMER TREND & COMPANY LTD PLYMOUTH

MADE IN ENGLAND

www.ingramcontent.com/pod-product-compliance
Lightning Source LLC
LaVergne TN
LVHW051804080426
835511LV00019B/3403